ZAP! I'm a Mind Reader

ZAP! I'm a Mind Reader

by Dan Greenburg
Illustrated by Jack E. Davis

ZAP! I'm a Mind Reader

Text copyright © 1996 by Dan Greenburg.
Illustration copyright © 1996 by Jack E. Davis.
All rights reserved.

First published in the United States by Grosset & Dunlap, Inc., a member of Penguin Putnam Books for Young Readers
under the title ZAP! I'M A MIND READER.

This Korean and English edition was published by Longtail Books, Inc. in 2020 by arrangement with Sheldon Fogelman
Agency, Inc. through KCC(Korea Copyright Center Inc.), Seoul.

ISBN 979-11-86701-57-7 14740

Longtail Books

I'd like to thank my editors,
Jane O'Connor and Judy Donnelly,
who make the process of writing and revising
so much fun, and without whom
these books would not exist.

I also want to thank
Jennifer Dussling and Laura Driscoll
for their terrific ideas.

For Judith, and for the real Zack,
with love—D.G.

Chapter 1

Have you ever wished you could read people's minds? **Tune** into their heads and hear **exact**ly what they're thinking? Well, forget it. You wouldn't like it. I know. I did it. And it wasn't a big **treat** at all. Believe me.

I guess I should begin at the beginning. My name is Zack. I'm ten years old. I live

in New York City. And I'm in the fifth
grade at the Horace Hyde-White School
for Boys.

Ever since I was young, I've been
interested in **weird stuff**. I don't think
I'm weird myself. But I keep wishing
that **alien**s would invite me onto their
spaceship. Or that I could **float** out of my
body and travel far away without stopping
at gas **station** restrooms, which are always
pretty **gross**.

Science is probably my favorite **subject**.
It teaches you stuff that is at least as weird
as reading minds. For example, do you
know what a tachyon[1] is? A tachyon is

---

1 **tachyon** 타키온. 과학 분야에서 사용하는 용어로, 크기가 아주 작고 빛
보다 더 빠르게 이동하는 가상의 입자를 가리킨다.

one of the **tiniest** things in the **universe**. Tinier than an atom,[2] even. And it travels faster than the speed of light. A tachyon travels so fast, it gets where it's going before it starts out. If you were a tachyon, you'd never be late to school. You'd get there before you left home. I learned that in science class.

The time I want to tell you about happened in science class. Mrs. Coleman-Levin is my science teacher. She's also my **homeroom** teacher.[3] She's kind of weird, but not in a bad way. For one thing, she always wears work **boot**s. Even in

---

2 **atom** 원자. 물질의 기본적 구성 단위. 하나의 핵과 이를 둘러싼 여러 개의 전자로 구성되어 있다. 눈으로 볼 수 없을 정도로 매우 작다.

3 **homeroom teacher** 담임 선생님. 홈룸(homeroom)은 미국 학교에서 학생들이 출석 확인이나 종례 등을 위해 모이는 교실을 말한다.

summer. Even at **dress-up** parties at school in the evening. For another thing, she works weekends at the **morgue**. She does autopsies.[4] That means cutting up dead people to see what they died of. Gross. But interesting.

Our classroom has a lot of weird, interesting stuff in it. There's a **complete** human **skeleton** hanging in the corner. Not a plastic model, either. It's a real one. On her desk, Mrs. Coleman-Levin keeps a glass **jar** with a pig **brain** in it. And we have lots of class **pet**s. But not the cute, **furry** kind. We have a piranha[5] fish and a tarantula[6] and a snake. The piranha eats

---

4 **autopsy** 부검(剖檢). 시신을 해부하여 사망의 원인을 검사하는 일.

goldfish.[7] The snake eats mice, which is kind of gross. Mrs. Coleman-Levin **feed**s them when we're not around. I don't think it **bother**s her at all.

On the day I want to tell you about, Mrs. Coleman-Levin was helping us do an **experiment**. It was with small **electric motor**s. I was **hook**ing one **up**. By **accident**, one of the **wire**s fell into a beaker[8] of water. Without thinking, I **reach**ed in and pulled it out. Suddenly my hand got all **tingly**. I felt as if **spark**s were

---

5 **piranha** 피라냐. 잉어목의 열대성 민물고기로 남아메리카의 아마존강 유역에 분포한다. 이빨이 강하고 사나워서 다른 고기를 잡아먹는다.

6 **tarantula** 타란툴라. 크기가 크고 무서워 보이나 독성은 약하며 아메리카 중남부와 아프리카 등지에 산다.

7 **goldfish** 금붕어. 붕어를 집에서 기를 수 있도록 작게 개량한 것으로 모양과 빛깔이 다른 많은 품종이 있다.

8 **beaker** 비커. 액체를 붓는 입이 달린 원통 모양의 화학 실험용 유리그릇.

shooting out of me.

"Zack!" Mrs. Coleman-Levin came rushing over to me. "Are you all right?"

"Uh, sure. Sort of," I said.

I really couldn't tell at that point, if you want to know the truth. I was too busy watching the little fireworks that were going off—Pop! Pop!—right in front of my eyes. Then I totally blacked out.

Chapter 2

"How are you feeling, **dear**?" said a strange, **echo**ey voice.

It was the school nurse,[1] Mrs. Krump. Her voice doesn't usually echo.

"Fine, thanks," I said. I always answer "Fine, thanks," even when I'm not. I've

---

1 school nurse 양호 선생님 또는 보건 교사. 미국 학교에서 학생의 건강
이나 위생에 대한 관리 및 지도를 하는 간호사를 말한다.

found that when people ask you how you are, they don't really want to know. They only want you to say you're fine so they can **get on to** the next thing.

"By the way," I said, "why am I here?"

"Don't you remember?" said Mrs. Krump in her echoey voice.

"Sure. Sort of," I said. "But tell me anyway."

"Well, you got an **electric** shock in science class," she said. "You put your hand in a beaker of water that had live **wire**s in it. It **knock**ed you **out**."

"Oh, right," I said. "I remember that."

And then a strange thing happened. Although her **lip**s didn't move, I thought I heard Mrs. Krump say, *Stupid **klutz**. You're* *lucky you didn't **electrocute** yourself.*

"Excuse me?" I said.

"What?" said Mrs. Krump.

"You just called me a stupid klutz."

Mrs. Krump's face turned bright red.

"I said no such thing," she replied. And then, although her lips weren't moving at all, I heard her say, *Must've been **muttering** **under my breath**. Better watch it.*

I don't know how she did it. Maybe she was a ventriloquist.[2]

"How did you do that?" I asked.

"How did I do what?"

"Say what you just said without moving your lips."

---

2 **ventriloquist** 복화술사. 입을 움직이지 않고 말하는 기술인 복화술 (ventriloquism)을 사용하는 사람.

Mrs. Krump **frown**ed. She gave me a **funny** look. She made me lie down for fifteen minutes. She stuck a **thermometer** in my mouth. Then she said, "Zack, you do not have any **fever**. And you don't seem to be **badly** hurt. Would you like to go on to your next class?"

"OK," I said.

If I had remembered what my next class was, I probably wouldn't have said OK.

Chapter 3

My next class was **geography**. I like geography a lot. But we were having this big test that day. And I forgot to take my geography book home with me to study. So I was pretty much **out of luck**.

Our geography teacher, Mr. Snodgrass, passed out **sheet**s with the test questions. I took a look at mine and started feeling

dizzy. The first question was, "Name the two biggest rivers in Iraq.[1]"

My heart **sank** like a stone. I didn't have a **clue**. I wasn't even sure what **continent** Iraq was in. Then suddenly a picture **pop**ped into my head. I had no idea where it came from. It was of a mother tiger with her **cub**s. And a **bunch** of kids were **nearby**, looking **scared**. The cubs kept **yell**ing, "You Fraidies![2]" at the kids.

What the heck[3] did that **have to do with** rivers in Iraq?

Then I heard a voice inside my head.

---

1 **Iraq** 이라크. 서아시아 남서부에 위치한 공화국으로, 수도는 바그다드이다.
2 **fraidy** 겁쟁이. 'afraid(두려워하는)'에서 나온 말로, 'fraidy cat'이라고도 한다.
3 **heck** '도대체', '젠장' 또는 '제기랄'이라는 뜻으로 당혹스럽거나 짜증스러운 감정을 강조하는 속어.

It said, *Tigress and you Fraidies.* **That was
it!** The two biggest rivers in Iraq were the
Tigris[4] and the Euphrates![5] But how did
I remember it? I quickly wrote down the
answers.

I looked at the second question. "What
is the tallest mountain in the world?" I
was about to skip it. But then the answer
popped inside my head again. Just like the
last time. *Mount Everest.*[6]

Wow! I was feeling great. I knew more
than I thought I did!

---

4 **Tigris** 티그리스강. 터키와 이라크에 걸쳐 흐르는 강으로, 그 길이는 약
   1,850킬로미터이며 유속이 매우 빠르다.

5 **Euphrates** 유프라테스강. 서아시아에서 가장 큰 강으로, 그 길이가 약
   2,800킬로미터에 달한다. 티그리스강과 함께 메소포타미아 지역을 흐르는
   주요 강이다.

6 **Mount Everest** 에베레스트산. 네팔과 티베트 사이에 있는, 세계에서 가
   장 높은 산. 높이가 약 8,848미터이며 산봉우리에는 항상 큰 빙하가 있다.

I went on to the next question. "**List** the continents of the world in order of size." Oh, boy.[7] I stopped feeling so smart. I knew Asia was pretty darn[8] big. And I knew that North America and South America were continents. But was Australia[9] a continent, or a really big island? And . . .

I didn't have to think any further. The voice in my head said, *Let's see . . . Asia, Africa, North America, South America, Antarctica,*[10] *Europe, and Austral—*

---

7 **boy** 여기에서는 '소년'이라는 뜻이 아니라, '맙소사!' 또는 '어머나!'라는 의미로 놀람이나 실망, 기쁨 등을 나타내는 표현으로 쓰였다.

8 **darn** 말하는 내용을 강조하기 위해 덧붙이는 속어로 '끝내주게' 또는 '빌어먹을'이라는 뜻으로 쓰인다.

9 **Australia** 오스트레일리아 대륙. 세계에서 가장 작은 대륙이자 세계에서 가장 오래된 대륙이다.

10 **Antarctica** 남극 대륙. 지구의 남쪽 끝에 있는 대륙으로, 기온이 몹시 낮아 땅의 대부분이 눈과 얼음으로 덮여 있다.

At that **exact** moment I heard a **snap**ping sound next to me. And the voice inside my mind said, *Darn pencil!* I turned around to see Spencer Sharp. He was holding a pencil with a broken point.

Spencer is the smartest kid in our class. He does math in his head that I can **barely** do on a **calculator**.

"Zack!" called out Mr. Snodgrass. "Eyes on our own papers, please!"

"Sorry," I said.

I sat back in my chair and **gulp**ed. The voice in my head **belong**ed to Spencer! I hadn't remembered all those answers. I'd heard Spencer the way I'd heard Mrs. Krump. And now I knew what was going on. It all had started with that electric

shock I got.

Holy guacamole![11] I could read people's minds!

This meant I'd been getting the test answers from Spencer Sharp. Not by looking at his paper, but by looking at his mind!

Question: Is reading somebody's mind **cheat**ing? I wasn't too sure about that. But just to **be on the safe side**, I decided not to listen anymore.

I tried **hum**ming. And I did my best to finish the rest of the test by myself. During a question on **ocean**s I hummed a Beach Boys[12] song. It was one my dad

---

11 holy guacamole '맙소사!', '이럴 수가!'라는 뜻으로 믿기 어렵거나 충격적인 일에 대해 놀라움을 표현하는 감탄사.

likes called "Catch a **Wave**.[13]" Still, I couldn't quite **drown** out the sound of Spencer's answers.

"Somebody appears to be humming," said Mr. Snodgrass. "Zack, is that you?"

"Uh, possibly," I said.

"Well, then, please be silent."

"Yes, sir," I said.

For a question about rain forests,[14] I hummed a song we used to sing in day **camp**.[15] "John Jacob Jingleheimer-

---

12 Beach Boys 비치 보이스. 1960년대부터 1980년대까지 많은 인기를 누린 미국의 5인조 록 그룹. 대표곡으로는 'Surfin' U.S.A.' 등이 있다.

13 Catch a Wave 비치 보이스가 1963년에 발매한 앨범에 수록된 곡. 1960년대에 유행한, 경쾌하고 서핑할 때 듣기 좋은 대중 음악인 서프 음악 (surf music)의 형식을 띠고 있다.

14 rain forest 우림(雨林). 연중 우량이 많고 습윤하게 유지되며 수목의 생육이 좋고 울창한 밀림이 조성된 숲.

15 day camp 주간 캠프. 어린이를 위해 낮에만 진행하는 야영 프로그램. 밤에는 집에 돌아간다.

Schmidt.[16]"

"Zack!" Mr. Snodgrass called out. "If you don't stop humming, you're going to have to give me your test paper now and leave the room."

"I'm sorry, sir," I said. "I won't do it anymore."

I tried to hum only in my head. But for the rest of the class, Spencer's thoughts kept **bleed**ing through my humming.

"OK, **time is up**," said Mr. Snodgrass.

I was pretty sure I had gotten an A. But I felt **funny** about it. I saw that this mind reading **stuff** could be trouble.

---

16 **John Jacob Jingleheimer-Schmidt** 미국의 전래 동요. 같은 가사를 소리나 속도를 다르게 하며 반복적으로 부르는 노래로, 보이스카우트 등의 어린이 단체에서 자주 부른다.

Just how much trouble, I was about to find out.

Chapter 4

School was almost over. I went into my classroom to get my **bookbag**. Mrs. Coleman-Levin was at her desk with the pig's **brain** on it. She had no idea I could read minds! I looked around the room at the other guys in the class. None of them knew my powers!

As I turned my head, it was like **tuning**

the **knob** on a radio. Little bits of what the kids were thinking came to me, **separated** by **static:**

. . . I can't believe how much homework I have . . .

. . . That pizza I had for lunch is still **stuck** *in my* **stomach** *. . .*

I couldn't tell who was thinking these things. But I knew it was all coming from kids in the room.

The door opened, and Floyd Hogmeister, the **janitor**, came in. The kids in my class are kind of **scare**d of him. You know how they say some people have eyes in the back of their heads? Well, that's Mr. Hogmeister. He doesn't miss a thing— especially if a kid is doing something he shouldn't.

"I heard you had some trouble with an **outlet**," he said to Mrs. Coleman-Levin.

"Yes, Floyd," she said. "Zack must have **short**ed it out earlier in the day when he got an **electric** shock. I think you might need to **replace** it."

"I'll have a **look-see**," he said.

The janitor went to check the outlet that **blew** up when I got **electrocute**d. While he was doing that, I **scan**ned the room. I was trying to **pick up** more **bits and pieces** of what people were thinking:

. . . *Mom said not to eat too much candy after school. Is a pound[1] too much? . . .*

---

1 **pound** 무게의 단위 파운드. 1파운드는 약 0.45킬로그램이다.

*. . . I'm going to get an F on that **geography** test. And Dad's going to go crazy . . .*

. . . Kill. Kill today? Kill now? No! Kill tomorrow! . . .

Whoa! What was this? Did I hear right? I **jiggle**d my head. Then I scanned the room again.

*. . . If I **ask** Spencer **over**, maybe he'll let me **copy** his homework . . .*

*. . . Is today the eighth day I've worn this **underwear**, or only the seventh? Tomorrow for sure I'll put on clean ones . . .*

. . . I love to kill. Can't kill now. Wait till tomorrow. Kill tomorrow! . . .

There it was again! Who was thinking this? I finished stuffing my books into my bookbag. Then I looked around the room. I tried to act **cool** about it. But those thoughts sounded like somebody was **plot**ting a **murder**. Could that be? Was one of the twenty kids in our class a crazy **psycho** killer?

No, I knew these guys. They might do stupid things, or even **gross** stuff. But kill somebody? **No way**.

Then my eyes **came to rest** on the janitor, Mr. Hogmeister. Hmmmm. He sure was **creepy**. But a murderer?

I had no idea whose thoughts I was picking up. But I was worried. I thought I better **check** this **out** with my teacher.

I went up to Mrs. Coleman-Levin's desk. She was **mark**ing some papers, **frown**ing.

"Could I speak to you a moment, Mrs. Coleman-Levin?" I asked.

She didn't look up from her **pile** of papers.

"I'm pretty busy now, Zack," she said.

"I'm sorry," I said. "It's kind of important."

She let out this really big **sigh**. Mrs. Coleman-Levin is not what you'd call a warm, **fuzzy** type.

"OK, **shoot**," she said.

I looked around. A lot of the kids were **staring** at me. So was Mr. Hogmeister. His eyes **fasten**ed on to me like *he* was reading *my* mind. And I **swear** I heard him say, *This is the kid who shorted out the outlet. Little **troublemaker**. I'd better watch* *him.*

I smiled weakly at Mr. Hogmeister. Then I turned back to Mrs. Coleman-Levin.

"Perhaps I could speak to you outside?" I said.

"Outside? Why outside?"

"Because what I have to say is **private**," I said.

"OK," she said. "Follow me."

She **clomp**ed outside the classroom in her work **boot**s. I followed her into the hall.

"What is it, Zack?"

"First, can I ask you a **personal** question, Mrs. Coleman-Levin?"

"**Depend**s what it is," she said.

"Do you believe in ESP?[2]"

"I don't know," she said. "I am a scientist. So I **have an open mind**. It's possible such things exist. Why do you ask?"

"Because I think today I learned how to read minds," I said.

"I see" was all she said.

"I've been listening to the thoughts of people in the classroom," I told her. "And I know this will sound **unbelievable**, but I think one of them is plotting a murder. Tomorrow!"

Mrs. Coleman-Levin looked at me very seriously.

---

2 **ESP** 'Extra-Sensory Perception(초감각적 지각)'의 약어. 사람의 감각기관을 통하지 않고서 외부세계를 지각하는 것을 말한다. 현대 과학으로는 설명할 수 없는 투시, 예지 등의 현상이 이에 속한다.

"You're telling me you read the mind of a murderer?" she said.

I **nod**ded. Then she took my hand and **pat**ted it. That is not like Mrs. Coleman-Levin at all.

From somewhere inside my head I heard, *This kid is **loony** toons!*[3] *Crazy as a bedbug.*[4]

"I'm glad you told me this, Zack," she said. She was giving me this really **sincere** smile. "Tomorrow, let's **keep our eyes and ears open**. Maybe together we can **discover** who it is and stop him before he kills."

---

3 **loony toons** (= looney tunes) '정신이 나간' 또는 '미친 사람'이라는 뜻의 속어.

4 **crazy as a bedbug** '제정신이 아닌'이라는 의미의 숙어.

"Sure," I said.

Mrs. Coleman-Levin didn't believe a word I'd said.

"But for now," she said, "get yourself back in that classroom."

We went back in. A minute later the bell rang and Mrs. Coleman-Levin **dismiss**ed us.

"OK, everybody. Good-bye," she said. "I'm off to the **morgue**. But first, it's **chow** time for the snake. And on the menu today is a nice **juicy** mouse."

Mrs. Coleman-Levin had this really happy look on her face.

Boy, what a **weirdo***!* I **overheard** one of the kids thinking as we **file**d out of **homeroom**. *She actually likes cutting up* *dead bodies.*

Hmmm. That got me thinking. Maybe Mrs. Coleman-Levin liked cutting up live bodies, too!

Chapter 5

When I got home, I decided to tell my dad what had happened. We've always been pretty close. But we've become even closer since my **folks** **split** up, and Dad got his own apartment. I can tell my dad anything at all. And he always understands.

"I don't understand," said my dad.

"You say you think you can read people's minds?"

"No, Dad," I said. "I don't *think* I can. I *know* I can."

"I'm sorry, Zack," he said, "but that doesn't seem possible."

"Oh, it's possible, all right," I said.

"OK then. What am I thinking right now? Right this very minute?"

"Here is what you're thinking," I said. "Maybe the **divorce** is finally **getting to** me. Maybe you ought to send me to that child **psychologist**."

His mouth dropped open.

"How did you know that's what I was thinking?" he **whisper**ed.

"Dad, I already told you," I said. "I read

minds. It happened in science class. I got an electric shock."

"OK, what am I thinking now?"

"You're hoping the psychologist is free next Monday," I said. "Dad, trust me. This **has nothing to do with** the divorce."

He **sigh**ed and shook his head.

"This is **amazing**," he said. "Truly amazing. OK, what number am I thinking of?"

"Eighty-seven," I said. "Dad, I need your advice about something I heard in school. Somebody is **plot**ting a **murder**."

He looked at me very seriously and **narrow**ed his eyes.

"What animal am I thinking of?" he asked.

"A duck-**bill**ed platypus,[1]" I said **impatient**ly. "Dad, didn't you hear what I said? *Somebody in school is plotting a murder.*"

"I'm sorry, Zack," he said. "It's just pretty **incredible** to find out your son is a mind reader. But you **nail**ed everything I was thinking. **Including** the eighty-seven and the duck-billed platypus. Now what's all this about somebody plotting a murder?"

"I **pick**ed **up** somebody's thoughts. They said they were going to kill someone. Tomorrow. I can't believe it could be one of the kids in my class. Maybe it's the **janitor**. He's very **weird**. Anytime we

---

1 **duck-billed platypus** 오리너구리. 주둥이가 오리의 부리처럼 길고 발가락에는 물갈퀴가 있다. 포유류로는 특이하게 알을 낳는다.

hang around his office in the basement,
he yells at us. Once he said if we didn't
stop bothering him, he'd kill us."

"Oh, that's just an expression," said my
dad. "People say that kind of thing all the
time. It doesn't mean they're killers."

Dad had a point. But if it wasn't Mr.
Hogmeister, who was it? Mrs. Coleman-
Levin?

"Dad, you've met Mrs. Coleman-Levin.
Did she strike you as the murdering
type?"

"Of course not. You're really being silly,
Zack," Dad said with a wave of his hand.
Then he focused his eyes on me. "OK,
now. What famous singer am I thinking of?
If you can do this every time, I could get

you on *The Tonight Show.*[2]"

I **tune**d Dad **out**. It was clear he wasn't taking this seriously. But then, he hadn't heard that **scary** voice saying, "Kill . . . Kill!" Somebody's life was in danger. And I was going to have to **solve** this **mystery** on my own. So far I had two main **suspect**s: Mr. Hogmeister and Mrs. Coleman-Levin.

And **in case** you're wondering which famous singer Dad was thinking of, it was Barry Manilow.[3] **Gross!**

---

2 **The Tonight Show** 투나잇 쇼. 1954년에 시작되어 지금까지 방송되고 있는 미국의 유명한 심야 토크 쇼로 세계에서 가장 오래 방송된 토크 쇼이다.

3 **Barry Manilow** 배리 매닐로. 1970년대 미국에서 많은 인기를 누린 유명 가수이자 작곡가. 그의 대표곡으로는 'Mandy', 'Copacabana' 등이 있다.

Chapter 6

I came to school wearing earmuffs[1] the next day. I looked stupid in them. But I found it helped **block** out other people's thoughts.

Here's the thing about mind reading. Most of the **stuff** you learn, you wish you

---

1 **earmuff** 귀마개. 귀가 시리지 않도록 귀를 덮는 방한 용품으로 털가죽 등으로 만든다.

hadn't. Like Mrs. Taradash, the old lady who lives next door to us. I learned she would like to have a date with my dad. I found that out this morning in the elevator. And Dad. I found out he hasn't been to the **dentist** in about two years. He makes me go every six months. It isn't **fair**!

I got to school half an hour early. That was so I could **snoop** around a little. It was **scary** having to **track** a killer by myself. But what else could I do? I couldn't go to the police. I mean what would I tell them? That I'd read the mind of somebody who was planning a murder? Somehow I didn't think they'd be too **impress**ed with that.

I took off my earmuffs, went down to the **basement**, and **hung around** the janitor's office. Mr. Hogmeister was my number-one **suspect**. That was mainly because I didn't want it to be Mrs. Coleman-Levin. She may be weird, but I like her.

I could hear the sounds of heavy rain and **thunder** outside. A big **storm** was **on its way**. I'd heard that on the morning news. It made the basement seem even scarier. But I didn't let that stop me. I had to find out who the killer was before he killed.

I **pretend**ed to be picking up **litter** in the **hallway**. But I was hoping to pick up **evil** thoughts from Mr. Hogmeister. For several minutes, Mr. Hogmeister didn't have a single interesting thought. *My nose itches,*

I heard. *I'll* **scratch** *it.* Then, *Mmmm, that feels good. Scratching is good. Especially if you itch. Not as good if you don't.* A second later I heard, ***Outlet.*** *Got to put in a new outlet. That kid Zack* **short***ed out the old one.* ***Dumb****!*

So Mr. Hogmeister thought I was dumb, did he? Well, I didn't think he was **exact**ly a **genius**. The question, though, was whether he was a killer.

I heard more thunder outside.

What was Mr. Hogmeister doing in there? I wished I could see. There was no **keyhole** in the door. But there was a little space between the door and the floor. I lay down and tried to **peer** under the door.

At first I didn't see anything at all. Then

I saw a huge pair of feet. Then the feet started walking toward the door! Oh, no! I had to get up fast!

The door **swung** open. I **scrambled** to my feet. But I **tripped** and **fell flat on my face**. Mr. Hogmeister stood over me like a **giant**.

Thunder **rumbled** closer.

"What the heck are you doing?" he said in this really angry voice.

"Oh, hi there, Mr. Hogmeister," I said. I got up and **slapped** the **dust** off my shirt and pants.

"I said, what were you doing down there on the floor in front of my office?" he **demanded**.

"Uh, push-ups,^{2} sir," I said.

"What?"

"I was doing push-ups. I always do push-ups before class. To sort of wake myself up."

Mr. Hogmeister **fasten**ed his scary eyes on me. Then he **lean**ed **way** down and pushed his face up close to mine. I think he must have eaten a garlic doughnut[3] for breakfast! P.U.[4]!

I was **scare**d he was going to take a **hammer** and **clonk** me over the head. But instead he did something else. He started laughing. I had never seen Mr. Hogmeister

---

2 **push-up** 팔 굽혀 펴기. 엎드린 자세에서 손을 바닥에 대고 팔을 굽혔다 폈다 하는 운동.

3 **doughnut** (= donut) 도넛. 밀가루를 반죽하여 고리 모양으로 만들어 기름에 튀긴 과자.

4 **P.U.** '웩', '어휴'라는 뜻을 지닌 감탄사 'phew' 또는 'pew'를 과장되게 나타낸 속어로 역겨움 등을 나타낼 때 사용한다.

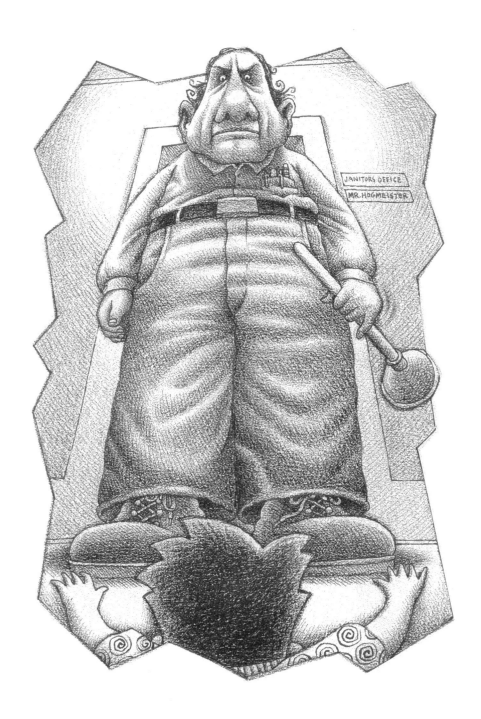

laugh before. It was not a pretty **sight**.

Then I **tune**d in on his thoughts. *Push-*

ups! ***Give me a break!*** *Does he really* ***expect***

me to believe that? He turned and walked

down the hallway, shaking his head. *These*

kids—they ***kill*** *me!* He laughed a weird

laugh again.

I watched Mr. Hogmeister go. I was

very **puzzle**d. His thoughts didn't exactly

sound like the thoughts of a murderer. Mr.

Hogmeister was a weird guy, all right. But

I was starting to think that maybe I should

cross him **off** my **list** of suspects. Only, if I

did that, then my number-one suspect was

. . . Mrs. Coleman-Levin!

Chapter 7

Outside my classroom, rain was **fling**ing
itself against the windows. **Lightning
flash**ed. **Thunder crash**ed. Mrs. Coleman-
Levin was taking **attendance**. And then
from somewhere I heard a strange voice.
Kill! Kill today!

Mrs. Coleman-Levin was finished with
attendance. Now she was standing up and

walking over to my desk. She was looking right at me. I heard, *Kill this one when the time is right! How I **crave** the **taste** of **blood**!*

Yikes!

"Zack," said Mrs. Coleman-Levin, "could you eat lunch quickly today? Then I want you to come right back up here to the classroom." There was a strange **expression** on her face.

"Uh, wh-what for?" I **stutter**ed.

"I need to talk to you."

"Alone, you mean?" I said, only it came out more like a **squeak**.

"Of *course* alone," she said. "I have a surprise for you."

I **swallow**ed hard. I had a feeling I knew what the surprise was. Mrs. Coleman-

Levin was a **psycho** killer, and I was her next **victim**. Some surprise! I had to get out of this. But how?

Between math and **geography** classes I tried to phone Dad. I wanted him to come and take me home. But when I called him, his answering machine[1] came on. Which is **weird**. My dad is always home. He's a writer, and that's where he works. But today, of all days, he was out. I left him a message. "Come and get me at school!" I said. "Right away!"

Then I went to Mrs. Krump's office. I told her I felt sick. If I stayed in her office, I'd be safe. But she took my **temperature**

---

1 **answering machine** 자동 응답기. 일정 시간 내에 전화를 받지 않으면 자동으로 작동하여 통화 내용을 녹음하는 기기.

and said there was nothing wrong with me. She sent me back up to English class.

At lunch I sat at Spencer Sharp's table. And I heard him thinking he'd invite me to his birthday party next month at Actionland **Amusement Park**. That would have been nice. Too bad I might not be **alive** to enjoy it.

Mrs. Coleman-Levin had told me to eat quickly. I was too scared to eat at all. The **storm** was really bad now. It was only 12:30. But it seemed as dark as night. And my dad hadn't shown up yet.

I was afraid to go **upstairs** to my classroom. But I had a plan. If Mrs. Coleman-Levin **pull**ed anything **funny**, I would **scream** and **run for my life**. OK, so this wasn't a great plan. It was just the best one I could think of under **pressure**. But when I got up to the room, Mrs. Coleman-Levin wasn't even there.

It was **creepy** being all alone in the classroom. In the corner, the **skeleton** seemed to be **grin**ning at me. Maybe once he'd been a student of Mrs. Coleman-Levin's, too.

I sat down at my desk to wait. There was a sudden **clap** of thunder. It was so loud I actually jumped a couple of inches[2] into the air. Right after that, all the lights **went out**.

Lightning must have **knocked out** the

---

2 inch 길이의 단위 인치. 1인치는 약 2.54센티미터이다.

power. I was pretty **freak**ed out, alone in the dark room.

Carefully I got up from my desk. From the flashes of lightning, I could almost see well enough to get to the door.

When I was about **halfway** there, I got this really creepy feeling. The feeling that I wasn't alone in the room. And right after that, I **pick**ed **up** a thought. It said, *There he is! Now I have him! The time to kill is now!*

Chapter 8

I screamed and rushed toward the door. Unfortunately, I tripped over a desk in the dark and came down hard on the floor. Pain shot through my knees.

Kill him! Kill him now! were the thoughts I heard in my ears.

Thunder exploded again outside. I started crying then. I have to admit it. I couldn't help it. You would have too, if you were me. If you don't think so, you're **kid**ding yourself.

And just then the lights **flicker**ed on. I **blink**ed in the **glare**. I looked around.

No one was there. Not a **soul**. So whose thoughts had I heard? I couldn't **figure** it **out**. Maybe I'd just imagined them. But just when I was beginning to think I was crazy, I heard them again. *He's **trapped**. Ready for the kill. **Swallow** him now!*

What? Wait a minute! *Swallow him?* What kind of killer could swallow a seventy-pound kid?

Out of the corner of my eye, I caught a quick **motion**. I turned and looked. Nothing. Just some fish in one of the

tanks. And then I looked again.

No, not just some fish. The piranha. The piranha **was about to** swallow a little fish! Mrs. Coleman-Levin must have put it in the piranha's tank at lunchtime. It was the piranha's thoughts I'd been **receiving** all along!

I **sprang** to the piranha tank. The piranha had trapped the little fish in the corner. With its **jaw**s wide open, it was about to **gulp** him down.

I **slap**ped the tank. Both fish jumped. I looked wildly around for a **fishnet**. Ah, there was one. I stuck it into the piranha tank and gently **scoop**ed up the little fish. Then I carried him to the fish tank and **plop**ped him into it. The water **splash**ed

my hand.

From somewhere I heard the **teeniest** voice I've ever heard. It said, *A **miracle**! A miracle! Saved by the hand of God!*

On the floor near the piranha tank was a **loose electric cord**. It ran the **filter motor** in the **aquarium**. It must have **yank**ed free when I slapped the tank to **distract** the piranha. I **bent** down and **plug**ged it back in. I forgot my hand was **wet**.

There was a blue **flash**. My hand **tingle**d all the way up my arm. **Firecracker**s **went off** in my eyes.

And then I **black**ed **out**.

Chapter 9

When I woke up, I was back on the **cot** in the nurse's office. Mrs. Krump and Mrs. Coleman-Levin were **staring** down at me. So was Dad.

"Oh, hi," I said.

"I found you on the floor of the classroom," said Mrs. Coleman-Levin. "How are you feeling?"

"Fine, thanks," I said. No, this time I'd tell the truth. "Actually, **not so hot**," I said.

"You gave us quite a **scare** there, Zack," said my dad.

"I'm sorry," I said. "Pretty **dumb** of me to **electrocute** myself twice, huh?"

"I'm glad you're OK," said Mrs. Coleman-Levin.

I **manage**d a smile. I was glad my **homeroom** teacher wasn't a **psycho** killer **after all**. I sat up.

"So what did you want to see me for?" I asked. "What was the surprise?"

"Oh, that," she said. "I decided to let a student **take care of** our tarantula over the vacation. I put everyone's name in a hat. And guess what? You won!"

"Uh . . . great . . . I guess," I said.

So that was the big surprise. Getting to take care of a tarantula. Well, it was better than getting killed by a psycho **murder**er.

"Good," said Mrs. Coleman-Levin. "I thought that would make you happy. The important thing, though, is that you're safe." She **pat**ted my hand again.

I waited to hear what she really thought. I heard nothing. What was going on here?

And then it **hit** me. Getting shocked a second time must have **knock**ed **out** my mind-reading powers. Was this possible? I had to **check** it **out**.

"Dad," I said, "think of a number between one and ten. Quick."

"OK, got it," he said. He turned to Mrs.

Krump and Mrs. Coleman-Levin. "Watch this," he said. "Zack can read minds. It's **amazing**."

"You're not serious," said Mrs. Krump.

"I'm **absolute**ly serious," said my dad. "Watch."

"The number you're thinking of is . . . five," I said.

"No," said my dad.

He looked at me and **frown**ed in **puzzle**ment.

"He usually gets it on the first guess," said my dad.

"The number you're thinking of is . . . ten."

"No," said my dad. He looked a little **embarrass**ed.

"The number you're thinking of is . . . three?"

"No," said my dad.

"One?"

"No."

"Seven?"

"No. Zack, what's going on?"

"Six?"

"No."

"Eight?"

"No. Zack, what's happening here?"

"Dad, I think my powers are gone," I said.

"You should have seen him yesterday," said my dad.

Mrs. Krump and Mrs. Coleman-Levin just **nod**ded. And even though I couldn't

pick up their thoughts, I'm pretty sure
they thought my dad and I were crazy.

So I'm not a mind reader anymore, and I
don't really miss it. Not that much, anyway.
Mind reading **complicate**s your life too
much. Now I'll just have to believe that
people really mean what they say.

And, since I can't pick up answers from
Spencer Sharp's mind anymore, I guess I'll
have to really study for the English test
next week.

ZAP! I'm a Mind Reader

by Dan Greenburg
Illustrated by Jack E. Davis

CONTENTS

The Zack Files • 4

Chapter 1
• Quiz & Words List ································· 10

Chapter 2
• Quiz & Words List ································· 18

Chapter 3
• Quiz & Words List ································· 22

Chapter 4
• Quiz & Words List ································· 28

Chapter 5
• Quiz & Words List ································· 38

Chapter 6
• Quiz & Words List ································· 44

Chapter 7
• Quiz & Words List ································· 52

Chapter 8
• Quiz & Words List ································· 58

Chapter 9
• Quiz & Words List ································· 66

번역 • 72
Answer Key • 90

THE ZACK FILES

평범한 소년이 겪는 기상천외하고 흥미로운 모험을 그린 이야기, 잭 파일스!

『잭 파일스(The Zack Files)』 시리즈는 뉴욕에 사는 평범한 소년, 잭이 겪는 때로는 으스스하고, 때로는 우스꽝스러운 모험을 담고 있습니다. 저자 댄 그린버그(Dan Greenburg)는 자신의 아들 잭에게서 영감을 받아서 그를 주인공으로 한 이야기를 떠올렸고, 초자연적인 현상에 대한 자신의 관심과 잭과 같은 아이들이 독서에 흥미를 갖길 바라는 마음을 담아서 책을 썼습니다.

그렇기 때문에 『잭 파일스』 시리즈는 누구나 한 번은 들어 본 기괴한 이야기를 아이들이 재미있게 읽을 수 있도록 흥미진진하게 소개합니다. 이 시리즈는 현재까지 총 30권의 책이 출간될 정도로 아이들의 호기심을 불러 일으켰고, 심지어 TV 드라마로도 제작되어 많은 관심과 사랑을 받았습니다.

이러한 이유로 『잭 파일스』 시리즈는 '엄마표 영어'를 하는 부모님과 초보 영어 학습자라면 반드시 읽어야 하는 영어 원서로 자리 잡았습니다. 간결한 어휘로 재치 있게 풀어 쓴 이야기는 원서 읽기에 두려움을 느끼는 학습자에게도 영어로 책을 읽는 재미를 선사할 것입니다.

퀴즈와 단어장, 그리고 번역까지 담긴 알찬 구성의 워크북!

이 책은 영어원서 『잭 파일스』 시리즈에, 탁월한 학습 효과를 거둘 수 있도록 다양한 콘텐츠를 덧붙인 책입니다.

- 영어원서: 본문에 나온 어려운 어휘에 볼드 처리가 되어 있어 단어를 더욱 분명히 인지하며 자연스럽게 암기하게 됩니다.
- 단어장: 원서에 나온 어려운 어휘가 '한영'은 물론 '영영' 의미까지 완벽하게 정리되어 있으며, 반복되는 단어까지 표시하여 자연스럽게 복습이 되도록 구성했습니다.
- 번역: 영어와 비교할 수 있도록 직역에 가까운 번역을 담았습니다. 원서 읽기에 익숙하지 않은 초보 학습자도 어려움 없이 내용을 파악할 수 있습니다.
- 퀴즈: 챕터별로 내용을 확인하는 이해력 점검 퀴즈가 들어 있습니다.

『잭 파일스』, 이렇게 읽어보세요!

● **단어 암기는 이렇게!** 처음 리딩을 시작하기 전, 해당 챕터에 나오는 단어를 눈으로 쭉 훑어봅니다. 모르는 단어는 좀 더 주의 깊게 보되, 손으로 쓰면서 완벽하게 암기할 필요는 없습니다. 본문을 읽으면서 이 단어를 다시 만나게 되는데, 그 과정에서 단어의 쓰임새와 어감을 자연스럽게 익히게 됩니다. 이렇게 책을 읽은 후에, 단어를 다시 한 번 복습하세요. 복습할 때는 중요하다고 생각하는 단어들을 손으로 쓰면서 꼼꼼하게 외우는 것도 좋습니다. 이런 방식으로 책을 읽다보면, 많은 단어를 빠르고 부담 없이 익히게 됩니다.

● **리딩할 때는 리딩에만 집중하자!** 원서를 읽는 중간 중간 모르는 단어가 나온다고 워크북을 들춰보거나, 곧바로 번역을 찾아보는 것은 매우 좋지 않은 습관입니다. 모르는 단어나 이해가 가지 않는 문장이 나온다고 해도 펜으로 가볍게 표시만 해두고, 전체적인 맥락을 잡아가며 빠르게 읽어나가세요. 리딩을 할 때는 속도에 대한 긴장감을 잃지 않으면서 리딩에만 집중하는 것이 좋습니다. 모르는 단어와 문장은, 리딩이 끝난 후에 한꺼번에 정리하는 '리뷰' 시간을 갖습니다. 리뷰를 할 때는 번역은 물론 단어장과 사전도 꼼꼼하게 확인하면서 왜 이해가 되지 않았는지 확인해 봅니다.

● **번역 활용은 이렇게!** 이해가 가지 않는 문장은 번역을 통해서 그 의미를 파악할 수 있습니다. 하지만 한국어와 영어는 정확히 1:1 대응이 되지 않기 때문에 번역을 활용하는 데에도 지혜가 필요합니다. 의역이 된 부분까지 억지로 의미를 대응해서 암기하려고 하기보다, 어떻게 그런 의미가 만들어진 것인지 추측하면서 번역은 참고 자료로 활용하는 것이 좋습니다.

● **2~3번 반복해서 읽자!** 영어 초보자라면 2~3회 반복해서 읽을 것을 추천합니다. 초보자일수록 처음 읽을 때는 생소한 단어와 스토리 때문에 내용 파악에 급급할 수밖에 없습니다. 하지만 일단 내용을 파악한 후에 다시 읽으면 어휘와 문장 구조 등 다른 부분까지 관찰하면서 조금 더 깊이 있게 읽을 수 있고, 그 과정에서 리딩 속도도 빨라지고 리딩 실력을 더 확고하게 다지게 됩니다.

- **'시리즈'로 꾸준히 읽자!** 한 작가의 책을 시리즈로 읽는 것 또한 영어 실력 향상에 큰 도움이 됩니다. 같은 등장인물이 다시 나오기 때문에 내용 파악이 더 수월할 뿐 아니라, 작가가 사용하는 어휘와 표현들도 자연스럽게 반복되기 때문에 탁월한 복습 효과까지 얻을 수 있습니다. 『잭 파일스』 시리즈는 현재 4권, 총 21,104단어 분량이 출간되어 있습니다. 시리즈를 꾸준히 읽다 보면 영어 실력도 자연스럽게 향상될 것입니다.

영어원서 본문 구성

내용이 담긴 본문입니다.
원어민이 읽는 일반 원서와 같은 텍스트지만, 암기해야 할 중요 어휘는 볼드체로 표시되어 있습니다. 이 어휘들은 지금 들고 계신 워크북에 챕터별로 정리되어 있습니다.

학습 심리학 연구 결과에 따르면, 한 단어씩 따로 외우는 단어 암기는 거의 효과가 없다고 합니다. 대신 단어를 제대로 외우기 위해서는 문맥(Context) 속에서 단어를 암기해야 하며, 한 단어 당 문맥 속에서 15번 이상 마주칠 때 완벽하게 암기할 수 있다고 합니다.

이 책의 본문은 중요 어휘를 볼드로 강조하여, 문맥 속의 단어들을 더 확실히 인지(Word Cognition in Context)하도록 돕고 있습니다. 또한 대부분의 중요한 단어는 다른 챕터에서도 반복해서 등장하기 때문에 이 책을 읽는 것만으로도 자연스럽게 어휘력을 향상시킬 수 있습니다.

또한 본문에는 내용 이해를 돕기 위해 '각주'가 첨가되어 있습니다. 각주는 굳이 암기할 필요는 없지만, 알아 두면 내용을 더 깊이 있게 이해할 수 있어 원서를 읽는 재미가 배가됩니다.

was. But there was nobody in **sight**.
I went on to a cage where a little tuxedo[2] kitten with a black body and white **paws** was taking a **nap**. h e sure was cute. I stopped to take a closer look at him. o f course, it probably wasn't the best time for me to **adopt** a kitten. In a couple of days my dad and I were flying to c hicago to spend t hanksgiving[3] with my Grandma Leah. But our **neighbor** had agreed to cat-sit.[4] a nd I wasn't **taking** any **chances** of my dad changing his mind.
I'd almost decided on that cute little

THE ZACK FILES

워크북(Workbook)의 구성

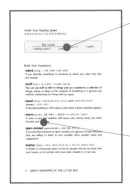

Check Your Reading Speed
해당 챕터의 단어 수가 기록되어 있어, 리딩 속도를 측정할 수 있습니다. 특히 리딩 속도를 중시하는 독자는 유용하게 사용할 수 있습니다.

Build Your Vocabulary
본문에 볼드 표시되어 있는 단어가 정리되어 있습니다. 리딩 전, 후에 반복해서 보면 원서를 더욱 쉽게 읽을 수 있고, 어휘력도 빠르게 향상됩니다.

단어는 〈빈도 – 스펠링 – 발음기호 – 품사 – 한국어 뜻 – 영어 뜻〉 순서로 표기되어 있으며 빈도 표시(★)가 많을수록 필수 어휘입니다. 반복해서 등장하는 단어는 빈도 대신 '복습'으로 표기되어 있습니다. 품사는 아래와 같이 표기했습니다.

n.명사 | a.형용사 | ad.부사 | v.동사
conj.접속사 | prep.전치사 | int.감탄사 | idiom 숙어및관용구

Comprehension Quiz
간단한 퀴즈를 통해 읽은 내용에 대한 이해력을 점검해 볼 수 있습니다.

번역
영문과 비교할 수 있도록 최대한 직역에 가까운 번역을 담았습니다.

이 책의 수준과 타깃 독자

- **미국 원어민 기준**: 유치원 ~ 초등학교 저학년
- **한국 학습자 기준**: 초등학교 저학년 ~ 중학생
- 영어원서 완독 경험이 없는 초보 영어 학습자 (토익 기준 450~750 점대)
- **비슷한 수준의 다른 챕터북**: Arthur Chapter Book, Flat Stanley, Magic Tree House, Marvin Redpost
- **도서 분량**: 약 5,000단어

아이도 어른도 재미있게 읽는 영어 원서를
<롱테일 에디션>으로 만나 보세요!

아서 챕터북 시리즈

플랫 스탠리 시리즈

Chapter
1

1. **What was Zack's opinion on reading people's minds?**

    A. It was a fantastic gift.

    B. It was not enjoyable.

    C. It was something everyone should try.

    D. It was not that difficult to do.

2. **Why did Zack like studying science?**

    A. He could memorize useful facts.

    B. He could learn about unusual things.

    C. He could make up his own experiments.

    D. He could act weird in class.

3. **What was NOT true about Mrs. Coleman-Levin?**

    A. She was Zack's science teacher.

    B. She had some strange qualities.

    C. She worked only as a teacher.

    D. She never wore fancy shoes.

4. **What did Zack's classroom contain?**

    A. Pets that were not typical

    B. A skeleton that was not real

    C. Glass jars that were full of candy

    D. A brain that was kept on Zack's desk

5. **Why did Zack's hand get tingly?**

    A. Zack set off a small explosion.

    B. Zack turned on an electric motor.

    C. Zack broke a large beaker.

    D. Zack touched a wet wire.

Check Your Reading Speed

1분에 몇 단어를 읽는지 리딩 속도를 측정해보세요.

$$\frac{519 \text{ words}}{\text{reading time ( ) sec}} \times 60 = (\quad) \text{ WPM}$$

Build Your Vocabulary

★ **tune** [tju:n] v. (채널을) 맞추다; 음을 맞추다; n. 곡, 선율; (마음의) 상태
To tune something means to adjust the controls on a radio or television so that you can receive a particular program or channel.

‡ **exact** [igzǽkt] a. 정확한; 꼼꼼한, 빈틈없는; 바로 그 (exactly ad. 정확히)
You use exactly to emphasize that something is correct in every way or in every detail.

‡ **treat** [tri:t] n. 즐거움을 주는 것, 기쁨; 대접, 한턱; v. 대접하다; (특정한 태도로) 대하다
A treat means a special and enjoyable occasion or experience.

‡ **grade** [greid] n. 학년; (상품의) 품질; 등급; v. (등급을) 나누다; 성적을 매기다
In the United States, a grade is a group of classes in which all the children are of a similar age.

★ **weird** [wiərd] a. 기이한, 기묘한; 기괴한, 섬뜩한
If you describe something or someone as weird, you mean that they are strange.

★ **stuff** [stʌf] n. 일, 것, 물건; v. 채워 넣다; 쑤셔 넣다
You can use stuff to refer to things such as a substance, a collection of things, events, or ideas, or the contents of something in a general way without mentioning the thing itself by name.

★ **alien** [éiljən] n. 외계인, 우주인; a. 이질적인; 외계의
In science fiction, an alien is a creature from outer space.

spaceship [spéisʃip] n. 우주선
A spaceship is a spacecraft that carries people through space.

⚹**float** [flout] v. (물 위나 공중에서) 떠가다; (물에) 뜨다; n. 부표
If something floats, it moves slowly and gently on water or in the air.

⚹**station** [stéiʃən] n. 장소; 부서; 역; v. 배치하다 (gas station n. 주유소)
A gas station is a place where you can buy fuel for your car.

⋆**gross** [grous] a. 역겨운; 아주 무례한; ad. 모두 (합해서)
If you describe something as gross, you think it is very unpleasant.

⚹**subject** [sʌ́bdʒikt] n. 과목; 연구 대상; 주제; a. ~에 달려 있는; v. 종속시키다
A subject is an area of knowledge or study, especially one that you study
at school, college, or university.

⚹**tiny** [táini] a. 아주 작은
Something or someone that is tiny is extremely small.

⚹**universe** [júːnəvəːrs] n. 세상; 우주; 은하계; (특정한 유형의) 경험 세계
The universe is the whole of space and everything in it, including the
earth, the planets and the stars.

homeroom [hóumrum] n. 생활 학급
In a school, homeroom is the class or room where students in the same
grade meet to get general information and be checked for attendance.

⋆**boot** [buːt] n. 목이 긴 신발, 부츠 (work boot n. 작업용 부츠)
Boots are shoes that cover your whole foot and the lower part of your
leg.

dress-up [drés-ʌp] a. 정장을 입어야 하는, 복장을 갖춰야 하는; n. 정장; 변장
In a dress-up party, you need to dress in formal clothes, or in clothes
more elegant than you usually wears.

morgue [mɔːrg] n. 시체 안치소, 영안실
A morgue is a building or a room where dead bodies are kept before
they are buried or burned, or before they are identified or examined.

‡ **complete** [kəmplíːt] a. 완전한; 완벽한; v. 완료하다, 끝마치다
If something is complete, it contains all the parts that it should contain.

⋆ **skeleton** [skélətn] n. 해골; 뼈대, 골격; (건물 등의) 골격
Skeleton is the set of bones that supports a human or animal body, or a model of this.

‡ **jar** [dʒaːr] n. (유리 등의) 병
A jar is a glass container with a lid that is used for storing food.

‡ **brain** [brein] n. 뇌
Your brain is the organ inside your head that controls your body's activities and enables you to think and to feel things such as heat and pain.

‡ **pet** [pet] n. 애완동물; v. (동물·아이를 다정하게) 어루만지다
A pet is an animal that you keep in your home to give you company and pleasure.

furry [fə́ːri] a. 털로 덮인; 털 같은
A furry animal is covered with thick, soft hair.

‡ **feed** [fiːd] v. 먹이를 주다; 먹여 살리다; 공급하다; n. (동물의) 먹이
If you feed a person or animal, you give them food to eat and sometimes actually put it in their mouths.

⋆ **bother** [báðər] v. 귀찮게 하다; 신경 쓰이게 하다; 신경 쓰다; n. 성가심
If something bothers you, it causes trouble or annoyance to you by interrupting or otherwise inconveniencing you.

‡ **experiment** [ikspérəmənt] n. 실험; 시험적인 행동; v. 실험을 하다
An experiment is a scientific test which is done in order to discover what happens to something in particular conditions.

⋆ **electric** [iléktrik] a. 전기의; 전기를 이용하는
An electric device or machine works by means of electricity, rather than using some other source of power.

motor [móutər] n. 모터, 전동기; a. 모터가 달린
The motor in a machine, vehicle, or boat is the part that uses electricity or fuel to produce movement, so that the machine, vehicle, or boat can work.

hook up idiom (전원·인터넷 등에) 연결하다
If you hook up something to a piece of electronic equipment or to a power supply, the two things are connected together.

accident [ǽksidənt] n. 우연; 사고, 사건 (by accident idiom 우연히)
If something happens by accident, it happens in a way that is not planned or organized.

wire [waiər] n. 전선; 철사; v. 전선을 연결하다
A wire is a long thin piece of metal that is used to fasten things or to carry electric current.

reach [riːʧ] v. (손·팔을) 뻗다; (손이) 닿다; ~에 이르다; n. (닿을 수 있는) 거리
If you reach somewhere, you move your arm and hand to take or touch something.

tingle [tiŋgl] v. 따끔거리다, 얼얼하다; n. 따끔거림; 흥분 (tingly a. 따끔거리는)
If something makes your body feel tingly, it gives you a feeling as if a lot of sharp points are being put lightly into your body.

spark [spaːrk] n. (전류의) 스파크; 불꽃, 불똥; v. 촉발시키다; 불꽃을 일으키다
A spark is a flash of light caused by electricity.

shoot [ʃuːt] v. 분출하다; 발사하다; 찌릿하다; int. 말해라
If you shoot something somewhere or if it shoots somewhere, it moves there quickly and suddenly.

rush [rʌʃ] v. 급히 움직이다; 서두르다; n. (감정이 갑자기) 치밀어 오름; 혼잡
If you rush somewhere, you go there quickly.

firework [fáiərwəːrk] n. (pl.) 불꽃놀이; 폭죽
Fireworks are small objects that are lit to entertain people on special occasions. They contain chemicals and burn brightly or attractively, often with a loud noise, when you light them.

go off idiom 터지다, 폭발하다; (경보기 등이) 울리다
If an explosive device or a gun goes off, it explodes or fires.

★**pop** [pap] n. 펑 (하는 소리); v. 펑 소리가 나다; 불쑥 나타나다; 눈이 휘둥그레지다
Pop is used to represent a short sharp sound, for example the sound
made by bursting a balloon or by pulling a cork out of a bottle.

black out idiom (일시적으로) 의식을 잃다
If you black out, you become unconscious or lose your memory for a
short time.

Chapter 2

1. How did Mrs. Krump's voice sound when Zack woke up?

A. It sounded loud.

B. It sounded normal.

C. It sounded odd.

D. It did not sound old.

2. Why did Zack tell Mrs. Krump that he was fine?

A. It was the only response he could think of.

B. It was an automatic answer.

C. He really did feel fine.

D. He did not want her to panic.

3. What did Zack hear Mrs. Krump say even though her lips were still?

   A. She hoped Zack would get better.

   B. She felt sorry for Zack.

   C. Zack was a careless fool.

   D. Kids like Zack were too childish.

4. What did Zack think of the situation?

   A. He assumed he was reading Mrs. Krump's mind.

   B. He figured Mrs. Krump was not actually saying anything.

   C. He thought maybe his hearing ability had become stronger.

   D. He wondered how Mrs. Krump talked without moving her mouth.

5. What did Mrs. Krump do before letting Zack leave?

   A. She had him rest for a bit.

   B. She asked him several questions.

   C. She scolded him for not being polite.

   D. She recommended that he go home.

Check Your Reading Speed

1분에 몇 단어를 읽는지 리딩 속도를 측정해보세요.

$$\frac{312 \text{ words}}{\text{reading time ( ) sec}} \times 60 = (\quad) \text{ WPM}$$

Build Your Vocabulary

dear [diər] n. 얘야; a. 사랑하는, 소중한; ~에게; int. 이런
You can call someone dear as a sign of affection.

echo [ékou] n. (소리의) 울림, 메아리; v. (소리가) 울리다 (echoey a. 울리는)
If you describe a sound as echoey, you mean that it is having or producing an echo or repeated sound by being reflected off a surface.

get on to idiom (새로운 주제로) 넘어가다
If you get on to something, you start talking about a different subject.

electric [iléktrik] a. 전기의; 전기를 이용하는 (electric shock n. 감전, 전기 충격)
If you get an electric shock, you get a sudden painful feeling when you touch something which is connected to a supply of electricity.

wire [waiər] n. 전선; 철사; v. 전선을 연결하다 (live wire n. 전기가 통하고 있는 전선)
A live wire is a wire that has electricity passing through it.

knock out idiom 기절시키다; ~을 쓸 수 없게 하다
To knock someone out means to cause them to become unconscious.

lip [lip] n. 입술
Your lips are the two outer parts of the edge of your mouth.

klutz [klʌts] n. 어설픈 사람, 얼뜨기
You can refer to someone who is very clumsy or who seems stupid as a klutz.

electrocute [iléktrəkjùːt] v. 감전 사고를 입히다; 감전사시키다
If someone is electrocuted, they are accidentally killed or badly injured when they touch something connected to a source of electricity.

mutter [mʌ́tər] v. 중얼거리다; 투덜거리다; n. 중얼거림
If you mutter, you speak very quietly so that you cannot easily be heard, often because you are complaining about something.

under one's breath idiom 작은 소리로; 소곤 소곤, 낮은 목소리로
If you say something under your breath, you say it in a very quiet voice, often because you do not want other people to hear what you are saying.

frown [fraun] v. 얼굴을 찡그리다; 눈살을 찌푸리다; n. 찡그림
When someone frowns, their eyebrows become drawn together, because they are annoyed or puzzled.

funny [fʌ́ni] a. 수상쩍은, 의심스러운; 이상한; 웃기는
If you describe something as funny, you think it is strange, unusual, or puzzling.

thermometer [θəːrmóumiːtər] n. 체온계; 온도계
A thermometer is a device used for measuring temperature, especially of the air or in a person's body.

fever [fíːvər] n. 열; 열기; 흥분, 초조
If you have a fever when you are ill, your body temperature is higher than usual and your heart beats faster.

badly [bǽdli] ad. 심하게; 몹시, 너무
If someone or something is badly hurt or badly affected, they are severely hurt or affected.

Chapter 3

1. **Why didn't Zack feel well in geography class at first?**

   A. He was unprepared to take his test.

   B. He disliked his teacher, Mr. Snodgrass.

   C. He had left his homework at home.

   D. Geography was his worst subject.

2. **How did Zack figure out the answers to the questions?**

   A. He looked at another student's paper.

   B. Another student said the answers out loud.

   C. The answers just entered his mind.

   D. He thought about what he had learned in class.

3. What did Zack notice about Spencer during class?

A. He was distracting all the students.

B. He broke the tip of his pencil.

C. He could not remember the names of places.

D. He was reading notes that he had written.

4. Why did Zack try not to listen to Spencer's voice?

A. He thought Spencer's voice was annoying.

B. He was confident he could do the test on his own.

C. He did not trust Spencer's answers.

D. He did not want to do something dishonest.

5. What happened when Zack hummed silently to himself?

A. He still heard Spencer's thoughts.

B. He could concentrate a little better.

C. He felt like time was going faster.

D. He forgot all about the test questions.

Check Your Reading Speed
1분에 몇 단어를 읽는지 리딩 속도를 측정해보세요.

$$\frac{693 \text{ words}}{\text{reading time ( ) sec}} \times 60 = (\quad) \text{ WPM}$$

Build Your Vocabulary

⁑**geography** [dʒiágrəfi] n. 지리학; (한 지역의) 지리, 지형
Geography is the study of the countries of the world and of such things as the land, seas, climate, towns, and population.

out of luck idiom 운이 나쁜, 운이 나빠서
If you are out of luck, you are unable to have or do something that you wanted.

⁎**sheet** [ʃiːt] n. (종이 등의) 한 장; 침대 시트, 얇은 천
You can use sheet to refer to a piece of paper which gives information about something.

⁎**dizzy** [dízi] a. 어지러운; (너무 변화가 심해) 아찔한
If you feel dizzy, you feel as if everything is spinning around you and that you are not able to balance.

⁑⁑**sink** [siŋk] v. (sank-sunk) 낙담하다, 풀이 죽다; 가라앉다, 빠지다; n. (부엌의) 개수대
If your heart sinks, you become depressed or lose hope.

⁎**clue** [kluː] n. 힌트; 실마리; (범행의) 단서 (**not have a clue** idiom 전혀 모르다)
If you do not have a clue about something, you do not know anything about it or you have no idea what to do about it.

⁎**continent** [kántənənt] n. 대륙; 육지
A continent is a very large area of land, such as Africa or Asia, that consists of several countries.

pop [pɑp] v. 불쑥 나타나다; 눈이 휘둥그레지다; 펑 소리가 나다; n. 펑 (하는 소리)
If something pops, it suddenly appears, especially when not expected.

★**cub** [kʌb] n. (곰·사자·여우 등의) 새끼, 어린 짐승
A cub is a young wild animal such as a lion, wolf, or bear.

★**bunch** [bʌnʧ] n. (사람의) 무리; 다발, 묶음; (양이나 수가) 많음
A bunch of people is a group of people who share one or more characteristics or who are doing something together.

★**nearby** [nìərbái] ad. 가까운 곳에; a. 인근의, 가까운 곳의
If something is nearby, it is only a short distance away.

‡**scare** [skɛər] v. 무서워하다; 놀라게 하다; n. 불안(감); 놀람, 공포 (scared a. 무서워하는)
If you are scared of someone or something, you are frightened of them.

★**yell** [jel] v. 고함치다, 소리 지르다; n. 고함, 외침
If you yell, you shout loudly, usually because you are excited, angry, or in pain.

have to do with idiom ~와 관련이 있다
If you have to do with someone or something, you are involved in or connected with them.

tigress [táigris] n. [동물] 암컷 호랑이
A tigress is a female tiger.

that is it idiom 바로 그것이다
You can use 'that is it' to say that something is correct.

be about to idiom 막 ~하려는 참이다
If you are about to do something, you are going to do it immediately.

★**skip** [skip] v. 건너뛰다, 생략하다; (일을) 거르다; 깡충깡충 뛰다; n. 깡충깡충 뛰기
To skip means to leave out something that would normally be the next thing that you would do.

★**mount** [maunt] n. 산; v. 올라가다; 증가하다
Mount is used as part of the name of a mountain.

‡list [list] v. (특정한 순서로) 열거하다; n. 명단, 목록
To list several things such as names means to write or say them one after another, usually in a particular order.

‡exact [igzǽkt] a. 바로 그; 정확한; 꼼꼼한, 빈틈없는
You use exact before a noun to emphasize that you are referring to that particular thing and no other, especially something that has a particular significance.

★snap [snæp] v. 딱 부러지다; 급히 움직이다; 딱 소리 내다; n. 탁 하는 소리
If something snaps or if you snap it, it breaks suddenly, usually with a sharp cracking noise.

★barely [béərli] ad. 간신히, 가까스로; 거의 ~아니게
When you can barely do something, you can do it in a way that is just possible but only with difficulty.

‡calculate [kǽlkjulèit] v. 계산하다; 추정하다 (calculator n. 계산기)
A calculator is a small electronic device that you use for making mathematical calculations.

gulp [gʌlp] v. (공포·놀라움에) 침을 꿀떡 삼키다; 꿀꺽꿀꺽 삼키다; n. 꿀꺽 마시기
If you gulp, you swallow air, often making a noise in your throat as you do so, because you are nervous or excited.

‡belong [bilɔ́ːŋ] v. ~에 속하다; 소속감을 느끼다
If something belongs to you, you own it.

‡cheat [ʧiːt] v. (시험 등에서) 부정행위를 하다; 속이다; n. 속임수
When someone cheats, they act in a dishonest way in order to gain an advantage, especially in a game, a competition, or an exam.

be on the safe side idiom 신중을 기하다, 조심하다
If you say you are doing something to be on the safe side, you mean that you are doing it in case something undesirable happens, even though this may be unnecessary.

hum [hʌm] v. 콧노래를 부르다, 흥얼거리다; 웅웅거리다; n. 웅웅거리는 소리
When you hum a tune, you sing it with your lips closed.

ocean [óuʃən] n. (태평양, 대서양 등) ~양; 대양, 바다
An ocean is one of the five very large areas of sea on the Earth's surface.

wave [weiv] n. 파도, 물결; 흔들기; v. 손짓하다; (손·팔을) 흔들다
A wave is a raised mass of water on the surface of water, especially the sea, which is caused by the wind or by tides making the surface of the water rise and fall.

drown [draun] v. (큰 소리로 작은 소리를) 안 들리게 하다; 익사시키다; 익사하다
(drown out idiom 안 들리게 하다)
If something drowns out a sound, it is so loud that you cannot hear that sound properly.

camp [kæmp] n. 캠프; 야영지, 텐트; 수용소; v. 야영하다
Camp is a place where people, especially children, can go to visit or live for a short time to enjoy nature or do organized activities.

bleed [bliːd] v. 번지다; 피를 흘리다; (물이나 공기를) 빼내다
To bleed means to spread from one area of something to another area.

time is up idiom 이제 시간이 다 됐다
If someone says time is up, it means the amount of time allowed to do or complete something is over.

funny [fʌni] a. 이상한; 수상쩍은, 의심스러운; 웃기는
If you feel funny, you feel slightly ill.

stuff [stʌf] n. 일, 것, 물건; v. 채워 넣다; 쑤셔 넣다
You can use stuff to refer to things such as a substance, a collection of things, events, or ideas, or the contents of something in a general way without mentioning the thing itself by name.

Chapter 4

1. What happened when Zack got to his classroom?

A. He heard only positive thoughts from the other kids.

B. He could not distinguish his thoughts from others' thoughts.

C. He could guess the other kids' thoughts by staring at them.

D. He heard thoughts but did not know who was thinking each one.

2. What was the janitor, Mr. Hogmeister, like?

A. He was afraid of people.

B. He was very alert.

C. He liked chatting with everyone.

D. He did not enjoy fixing things.

3. How did Zack feel when he heard the thought about killing?

A. He felt like he should just ignore it.

B. He felt like no one was in any real danger.

C. He felt like it must have been a joke.

D. He felt like it was not one of his classmates' thoughts.

4. What did Zack NOT tell Mrs. Coleman-Levin?

A. He still felt sick from the electric shock.

B. He had been reading minds.

C. Someone might be planning to kill.

D. A murder could occur the next day.

5. How did Mrs. Coleman-Levin react to what Zack said?

A. She acted unconcerned but was actually terrified.

B. She acted shocked but was actually feeling calm.

C. She acted supportive but was actually not convinced.

D. She acted confused but was actually not listening.

Check Your Reading Speed

1분에 몇 단어를 읽는지 리딩 속도를 측정해보세요.

$$\frac{1,005 \text{ words}}{\text{reading time ( ) sec}} \times 60 = (\qquad) \text{ wPM}$$

Build Your Vocabulary

bookbag [búkbæg] n. 책가방
A bookbag is a bag or satchel used especially by a student for carrying books.

복습 **brain** [brein] n. 뇌
Your brain is the organ inside your head that controls your body's activities and enables you to think and to feel things such as heat and pain.

복습 **tune** [tjuːn] v. (채널을) 맞추다; 음을 맞추다; n. 곡, 선율; (마음의) 상태
To tune something means to adjust the controls on a radio or television so that you can receive a particular program or channel.

★ **knob** [nab] n. (동그란) 손잡이; 혹, 마디
A knob is a round switch on a piece of machinery or equipment.

‡ **separate** [sépərèit] v. 분리하다, 나누다; 갈라지다; a. 별개의; 분리된
To separate means to divide into different parts or groups.

★ **static** [stǽtik] n. (수신기의) 잡음; 정전기; a. 고정된; 정지 상태의
If there is static on the radio or television, you hear a series of loud noises which spoils the sound.

stuck [stʌk] a. 움직일 수 없는, 꼼짝 못하는; 갇힌
If something is stuck in a particular position, it is fixed tightly in this position and is unable to move.

stomach [stʌ́mək] n. 위(胃), 복부, 배
Your stomach is the organ inside your body where food is digested before it moves into the intestines.

janitor [dʒǽnitər] n. (건물의) 관리인, 잡역부; 수위
A janitor is a person employed to take care of a large building, such as a school, and who deals with the cleaning or repairs.

scare [skɛər] v. 무서워하다; 놀라게 하다; n. 불안(감); 놀람, 공포 (scared a. 무서워하는)
If you are scared of someone or something, you are frightened of them.

outlet [áutlet] n. 콘센트; (액체·기체의) 배출구
An outlet is a place, usually in a wall, where you can connect electrical devices to the electricity supply.

short [ʃɔːrt] v. (전기 회로 등을) 합선시키다; a. 짧은; 부족한
If an electrical device is shorted out, a wrong connection or damaged wire causes electricity to travel along the wrong route and damage the device.

electric [iléktrik] a. 전기의; 전기를 이용하는 (electric shock n. 감전, 전기 충격)
If you get an electric shock, you get a sudden painful feeling when you touch something which is connected to a supply of electricity.

replace [ripléis] v. 교체하다; 대신하다, 대체하다
If you replace something that is broken, damaged, or lost, you get a new one to use instead.

look-see [lúk-siː] n. 잠깐 봄
If you have a look-see, you take a quick look or inspection.

blow [blou] v. (blew-blown) (퓨즈가) 나가다; 폭파하다; (입으로) 불다; n. 강타
If something electrical blows, it stops working, usually because too much electricity has passed through it.

electrocute [iléktrəkjùːt] v. 감전 사고를 입히다; 감전사시키다
If someone is electrocuted, they are accidentally killed or badly injured when they touch something connected to a source of electricity.

★ **scan** [skæn] v. (유심히) 살피다; 훑어보다; 정밀 촬영하다; n. 정밀 검사
When you scan a place or group of people, you look at it carefully, usually because you are looking for something or someone.

pick up idiom (어떤 정보를) 알게 되다; ~을 집어 올리다, 줍다
If you pick up interesting or useful information, you learn it from someone or something.

bits and pieces idiom 이런저런 것들, 잡동사니
You can use bits and pieces to refer to a collection of different things.

복습 **geography** [dʒiágrəfi] n. 지리학; (한 지역의) 지리, 지형
Geography is the study of the countries of the world and of such things as the land, seas, climate, towns, and population.

jiggle [dʒigl] v. 흔들다, (빠르게) 움직이다
If you jiggle something, you move it quickly up and down or from side to side.

ask over idiom ~을 집으로 초대하다
If you ask someone over, you invite them to come and visit you in your home.

복습 **copy** [kápi] v. (남의 숙제나 답안을) 베끼다; 복사하다; n. 복사; (책 등의) 한 부
If you copy a piece of writing, you write it again exactly.

★ **underwear** [Ándərwèr] n. 속옷
Underwear is clothing such as vests and pants which you wear next to your skin under your other clothes.

복습 **cool** [ku:l] a. 차분한, 침착한; 시원한; 멋진
If you say that a person or their behavior is cool, you mean that they are calm and unemotional, especially in a difficult situation.

★ **plot** [plat] v. 음모하다; (소설 등의) 구성을 짜다; n. (소설·영화 등의) 구성; 음모
If people plot to do something or plot something that is illegal or wrong, they plan secretly to do it.

‡**murder** [mə́:rdər] n. 살해, 살인죄; v. 살해하다, 살인하다
Murder is the deliberate and illegal killing of a person.

psycho [sáikou] n. (아주 이상하게 폭력적인) 정신병자; a. 정신병의; 정신 의학의
A psycho is someone who has serious mental problems and who may
act in a violent way without feeling sorry for what they have done.

복습 **gross** [grous] a. 역겨운; 아주 무례한; ad. 모두 (합해서)
If you describe something as gross, you think it is very unpleasant.

no way idiom 말도 안 돼; 절대로 안 되다; 싫어
You can say no way to tell someone that something is impossible.

come to rest idiom 멈춰 서다
if your eyes come to rest on someone or something, they look at that
person or thing and stop looking around at different people or things.

creepy [krí:pi] a. 기분 나쁜, 오싹한
If you say that someone or something is creepy, you mean they are
strange or unnatural, making you feel frightened.

check out idiom ~을 확인하다; 살펴보다
If you check out something or someone, you find out information about
them to make sure that everything is correct or satisfactory.

‡**mark** [ma:rk] v. (시험지 등을) 채점하다, (과제물을) 검사하다; 표시하다; n. 점수; 표시
When a teacher marks a student's work, the teacher decides how good
it is and writes a number or letter on it to indicate this opinion.

복습 **frown** [fraun] v. 얼굴을 찡그리다, 눈살을 찌푸리다; n. 찡그림, 찌푸림
When someone frowns, their eyebrows become drawn together, because
they are annoyed or puzzled.

‡**pile** [pail] n. 쌓아 놓은 것, 더미; 무더기; v. (차곡차곡) 쌓다; 우르르 가다
A pile of things is a quantity of things that have been put neatly
somewhere so that each thing is on top of the one below.

*sigh [sai] n. 한숨; v. 한숨을 쉬다; 탄식하듯 말하다
When you let out a sigh, you let out a deep breath, as a way of expressing feelings such as disappointment, tiredness, or pleasure.

fuzzy [fʌ́zi] a. 푸근한; 솜털이 보송보송한; 흐릿한, 어렴풋한
If you describe someone as fuzzy, you mean that they are full of love and kindness.

복습 shoot [ʃuːt] int. 말해라; v. 분출하다; 발사하다; 찌릿하다
You can use 'shoot' for telling someone to say what they want to say.

*stare [stɛər] v. 빤히 쳐다보다, 응시하다; n. 빤히 쳐다보기, 응시
If you stare at someone or something, you look at them for a long time.

*fasten [fæsn] v. (시선을 오랫동안) 고정시키다; 매다, 채우다; (단단히) 잠그다
If your eyes fasten on someone or something, you look at them for a long time.

복습 swear [swɛər] v. 장담하다; 맹세하다; 욕하다
If you say that you swear that something is true or that you can swear to it, you are saying very firmly that it is true.

troublemaker [trʌ́blmèikər] n. 말썽꾸러기
If you refer to someone as a troublemaker, you mean that they cause unpleasantness, quarrels, or fights.

복습 private [práivət] a. 사적인; 비공개의; 개인 소유의; 사생활의
Private meetings, discussions, and other activities involve only a small number of people, and very little information about them is given to other people.

clomp [klamp] v. 쿵쿵 걷다, 무거운 발걸음으로 걷다; n. 쿵 (하는 소리)
If someone clomps somewhere, they walk there heavily or noisily.

복습 boot [buːt] n. 목이 긴 신발, 부츠 (work boot n. 작업용 부츠)
Boots are shoes that cover your whole foot and the lower part of your leg.

* personal [pɔ́rsənl] a. 개인적인, 개인의
A personal opinion, quality, or thing belongs or relates to one particular person rather than to other people.

** depend [dipénd] v. ~에 좌우되다, 달려 있다; 의존하다, 의지하다
You use depend in expressions such as it depends to indicate that you cannot give a clear answer to a question because the answer will be affected or determined by other factors.

have an open mind idiom (~에 대해) 열린 태도를 갖다
If you have an open mind, you avoid forming an opinion or making a decision until you know all the facts.

unbelievable [ʌnbilíːvəbl] a. 믿기 힘든; 믿기 어려울 정도인
If an idea or statement is unbelievable, it seems so unlikely to be true that you cannot believe it.

* nod [nad] v. (고개를) 끄덕이다, 까딱하다; n. 끄덕임
If you nod, you move your head downward and upward to show that you are answering 'yes' to a question, or to show agreement, understanding, or approval.

* pat [pæt] v. 토닥거리다, 쓰다듬다; n. 토닥거리기, 쓰다듬기
If you pat something or someone, you tap them lightly, usually with your hand held flat.

loony [lúːni] a. 미친, 이상한; n. 괴짜
If you describe someone's behavior or ideas as loony, you mean that they seem mad or strange.

bedbug [bédbʌg] n. [곤충] 빈대
A bedbug is a small insect with a round body and no wings which lives in dirty houses and feeds by biting people and sucking their blood when they are in bed.

* sincere [sinsíər] a. 진심 어린, 진실된, 진정한; 진심의
Sincere words, feelings, or ways of behaving are true and honest.

keep one's eyes and ears open idiom 정신 바짝 차리고 조심하다
If you keep your eyes and ears open, you keep looking and listening so
that you will notice anything that is important or dangerous.

discover [diskʌ́vər] v. 알아내다, 찾다; 발견하다; 발굴하다
If you discover something, you find out about it or find some information
about it.

dismiss [dismís] v. (사람을) 보내다, 해산시키다; 묵살하다
If you dismiss someone, you send them away or allow them to leave.

morgue [mɔːrg] n. 시체 안치소, 영안실
A morgue is a building or a room where dead bodies are kept before
they are buried or cremated, or before they are identified or examined.

chow [tʃau] n. 음식 (chow time n. 식사 시간)
Chow time is the time for eating a meal.

juicy [dʒúːsi] a. 즙이 많은; 재미있는; 매력적인
If food is juicy, it has a lot of juice in it and is very enjoyable to eat.

weirdo [wíərdou] n. 괴짜, 별난 사람
If you describe someone as a weirdo, you disapprove of them because
they behave in an unusual way which you find difficult to understand
or accept.

overhear [òuvərhír] v. (overheard-overheard) (남의 대화 등을) 우연히 듣다
If you overhear someone, you hear what they are saying when they are
not talking to you and they do not know that you are listening.

file [fail] v. 줄지어 가다; (문서 등을) 보관하다; n. 파일, 서류철
When a group of people files somewhere, they walk one behind the
other in a line.

homeroom [hóumrum] n. 생활 학급
In a school, homeroom is the class or room where students in the same
grade meet to get general information and be checked for attendance.

Chapter 5

1. **Why did Zack decide to tell his dad everything?**

   A. He had no one else to talk to.

   B. He and his dad had a strong relationship.

   C. His dad knew he would never lie.

   D. His dad already thought mind reading was possible.

2. **What did Zack's dad think at first?**

   A. Zack was having a hard time because of his parents' divorce.

   B. Zack wanted to discuss his parents' divorce with his mom and dad.

   C. A child psychologist would be able to tell if Zack could read minds.

   D. A child psychologist could help Zack read minds more accurately.

3. Why did Zack's dad keep asking Zack to read his mind?

   A. He had nothing better to do.

   B. He hoped it would cheer Zack up.

   C. He was amazed by Zack's ability.

   D. He wanted to avoid discussing a murder.

4. How did Zack's dad react when Zack mentioned the janitor?

   A. He claimed a janitor could never hurt people.

   B. He agreed the janitor was probably the killer.

   C. He warned Zack to stay away from the janitor.

   D. He did not assume the janitor was a suspect.

5. What did Zack have to do?

   A. He had to find someone who would believe him.

   B. He had to contact the police about the killer.

   C. He had to find the killer by himself.

   D. He had to get his classmates to help him.

Check Your Reading Speed

1분에 몇 단어를 읽는지 리딩 속도를 측정해보세요.

$$\frac{537 \text{ words}}{\text{reading time (} \quad \text{) sec}} \times 60 = (\quad) \text{ WPM}$$

Build Your Vocabulary

⚡folk [fouk] n. (pl.) 부모, 가족; 사람들; 여러분; a. 민속의, 전통적인
You can refer to your close family, especially your mother and father, as your folks.

⚡split [split] v. (split-split) 헤어지다; 분열되다; 나뉘다; n. 분열; 분할
(**split up** idiom 헤어지다)
If two people split up, they end their relationship or marriage.

⚡divorce [divɔ́:rs] n. 이혼; v. 이혼하다
A divorce is the formal ending of a marriage by law.

get to idiom ~에게 영향을 미치다, 괴롭히다
If someone or something gets to you, they begin to annoy, upset, or affect you.

⚡psychology [saikálədʒi] n. 심리, 심리학 (**child psychologist** n. 아동 심리학자)
Child psychologists assess children and adolescents and help them cope with stresses or a variety of developmental issues.

⚡whisper [hwíspər] v. 소곤거리다, 속삭이다; n. 소곤거리는 소리, 속삭임
When you whisper, you say something very quietly, using your breath rather than your throat, so that only one person can hear you.

have nothing to do with idiom ~와 관련이 없다
When you have nothing to do with someone or something, you have no connection or influence with them.

^{복습}**sigh** [sai] v. 한숨을 쉬다; 탄식하듯 말하다; n. 한숨
When you sigh, you let out a deep breath, as a way of expressing feelings such as disappointment, tiredness, or pleasure.

✦ **amaze** [əméiz] v. (대단히) 놀라게 하다; 경악하게 하다 (amazing a. 놀라운)
You say that something is amazing when it is very surprising and makes you feel pleasure, approval, or wonder.

^{복습}**plot** [plat] v. 음모하다; (소설 등의) 구성을 짜다; n. (소설·영화 등의) 구성; 음모
If people plot to do something or plot something that is illegal or wrong, they plan secretly to do it.

^{복습}**murder** [mə́:rdər] n. 살해, 살인죄; v. 살해하다, 살인하다
Murder is the deliberate and illegal killing of a person.

^{복습}**narrow** [nǽrou] v. (눈을) 찌푸리다; 좁히다; a. 좁은
If your eyes narrow or if you narrow your eyes, you almost close them, for example because you are angry or because you are trying to concentrate on something.

✦ **bill** [bil] n. (새의) 부리; 청구서; 계산서 (-billed a. (~한) 부리가 있는)
You can combine '-billed' with adjectives to indicate that a bird has a beak of a particular kind or appearance.

✦ **impatient** [impéiʃənt] a. 짜증난, 안달하는 (impatiently ad. 조바심을 내며)
If you are impatient, you are annoyed because you have to wait too long for something.

✦ **incredible** [inkrédəbl] a. 믿을 수 없는, 믿기 힘든
If you say that something is incredible, you mean that it is very unusual or surprising, and you cannot believe it is really true, although it may be.

✦ **nail** [neil] v. ~을 완벽하게 하다; 못으로 박다; n. 손톱; 못
If you nail something, you do it extremely well or successfully.

✦ **include** [inklú:d] v. 포함하다; ~을 (~에) 포함시키다
You use including to introduce examples of people or things that are part of the group of people or things that you are talking about.

^복_습 **pick up** idiom (어떤 정보를) 알게 되다; ~을 집어 올리다, 줍다
If you pick up interesting or useful information, you learn it from someone or something.

^복_습 **janitor** [dʒǽnitər] n. (건물의) 관리인, 잡역부; 수위
A janitor is a person employed to take care of a large building, such as a school, and who deals with the cleaning or repairs.

^복_습 **weird** [wiərd] a. 기이한, 기묘한; 기괴한, 섬뜩한
If you describe something or someone as weird, you mean that they are strange.

hang around idiom ~에서 서성거리다
If you hang around, you stay in the same place doing nothing, usually because you are waiting for something or someone.

＊ **basement** [béismənt] n. (건물의) 지하층
The basement of a building is a floor built partly or completely below ground level.

^복_습 **yell** [jel] v. 고함치다, 소리 지르다; n. 고함, 외침
If you yell, you shout loudly, usually because you are excited, angry, or in pain.

^복_습 **bother** [báðər] v. 귀찮게 하다; 신경 쓰이게 하다; 신경 쓰다; n. 성가심
If something bothers you, it causes trouble or annoyance to you by interrupting or otherwise inconveniencing you.

＊ **expression** [ikspréʃən] n. 표현, 어구; 표정
An expression is a word or phrase.

have a point idiom 일리가 있다
If you say that someone has a point, you mean that you accept that what they have said is important and should be considered.

＊＊ **strike** [straik] v. ~하다는 인상을 주다; 치다, 부딪치다; n. 치기, 때리기
If something strikes you as being a particular thing, it gives you the impression of being that thing.

silly [síli] a. 어리석은, 바보 같은; 우스꽝스러운; n. 바보
If you say that someone or something is silly, you mean that they are foolish, childish, or ridiculous.

wave [weiv] n. (팔이나 손을) 흔들기; 파도, 물결; v. 손짓하다; 흔들다
A wave is a movement of your raised hand from side to side or up and down.

focus [fóukəs] v. 초점을 맞추다; 집중하다; n. 초점, 중심; 주목
If you focus your eyes or if your eyes focus, your eyes adjust so that you can clearly see the thing that you want to look at.

tune out idiom 듣지 않다, 무시하다
If you tune someone out, you stop listening or paying attention to what they are saying.

scary [skéəri] a. 무서운, 겁나는
Something that is scary is rather frightening.

solve [salv] v. (수학 문제 등을) 해결하다, 풀다; (곤경을) 해결하다
If you solve a mystery or a puzzle, you find the reason or explanation for it.

mystery [místəri] n. 수수께끼, 미스터리; 신비스러운 것
A mystery is something that is not understood or known about.

suspect [sʌ́spekt] n. 용의자; v. 의심하다; 수상쩍게 여기다
A suspect is a person who is believed to be guilty of something.

in case idiom ~할 경우에 대비해서
If you do something in case or just in case a particular thing happens, you do it because that thing might happen.

gross [grous] a. 역겨운; 아주 무례한; ad. 모두 (합해서)
If you describe something as gross, you think it is very unpleasant.

Chapter 6

1. Why did Zack wear earmuffs to school?

A. He thought they looked cool.

B. He wanted to fit in with the other kids.

C. The earmuffs stopped him from reading minds.

D. The earmuffs kept him warm in the cold weather.

2. Why did Zack go to school early?

A. So that he could look for clues

B. So that he would not get stuck in the storm

C. So that he could speak to his suspects

D. So that he would not be seen wearing earmuffs

3. **What happened when Zack went down to the basement?**
   A. He heard Mr. Hogmeister talking on the phone.
   B. He heard Mr. Hogmeister thinking boring thoughts.
   C. He saw Mr. Hogmeister cleaning up his office.
   D. He saw Mr. Hogmeister doing something suspicious.

4. **What did Zack attempt to do in the basement?**
   A. Lock Mr. Hogmeister in his office
   B. Watch Mr. Hogmeister from under his door
   C. Find the key to Mr. Hogmeister's office
   D. Open Mr. Hogmeister's door quietly

5. **Why did Mr. Hogmeister laugh at Zack?**
   A. He thought it was funny that Zack looked scared.
   B. He did not believe Zack knew how to exercise.
   C. He thought Zack did push-ups in a funny way.
   D. He did not believe Zack had been doing push-ups.

Check Your Reading Speed

1분에 몇 단어를 읽는지 리딩 속도를 측정해보세요.

$$\frac{720 \text{ words}}{\text{reading time ( ) sec}} \times 60 = (\qquad) \text{ wPM}$$

Build Your Vocabulary

‡ block [blak] v. 차단하다; 방해하다; n. 구역, 블록 (block out idiom (빛·소리를) 차단하다)
To block out means to stop light or sound from reaching something.

복습 stuff [stʌf] n. 일, 것, 물건; v. 채워 넣다; 쑤셔 넣다
You can use stuff to refer to things such as a substance, a collection of things, events, or ideas, or the contents of something in a general way without mentioning the thing itself by name.

★ dentist [déntist] n. 치과; 치과 의사
The dentist or the dentist's is used to refer to the place where a dentist carries out their job, which is examining and treating people's teeth.

‡ fair [fɛər] a. 공평한; 타당한; ad. 공정하게, 타당하게; n. 축제; 박람회
Something or someone that is fair is reasonable, right, and just.

snoop [snuːp] v. 기웃거리다, 염탐하다; n. 염탐꾼; 염탐
If someone snoops around a place, they secretly look around it in order to find out things.

복습 scary [skéəri] a. 무서운, 겁나는
Something that is scary is rather frightening.

‡ track [træk] v. 추적하다; 뒤쫓다; n. 자국; 경주로, 트랙; 길
If you track someone or something, you investigate them, because you are interested in finding out more about them.

★ **impress** [imprés] v. 깊은 인상을 주다, 감동을 주다 (impressed a. 인상 깊게 생각하는)
If you are impressed, you admire someone or something very much, especially because of an unusually good achievement, quality, or skill.

복습 **basement** [béismənt] n. (건물의) 지하층
The basement of a building is a floor built partly or completely below ground level.

복습 **hang around** idiom ~에서 서성거리다
If you hang around, you stay in the same place doing nothing, usually because you are waiting for something or someone.

복습 **janitor** [dʒǽnitər] n. (건물의) 관리인, 잡역부; 수위
A janitor is a person employed to take care of a large building, such as a school, and who deals with the cleaning or repairs.

복습 **suspect** [sʌ́spekt] n. 용의자; v. 의심하다; 수상쩍게 여기다
A suspect is a person who is believed to be guilty of something.

★ **thunder** [θʌ́ndər] n. 천둥; 천둥 같은 소리; v. 천둥이 치다; 우르릉거리다
Thunder is the loud noise that you hear from the sky after a flash of lightning, especially during a storm.

‡ **storm** [stɔːrm] n. 폭풍, 폭풍우; v. 기습하다; 쿵쾅대며 가다
A storm is very bad weather, with heavy rain, strong winds, and often thunder and lightning.

on one's way idiom 가까워져 오는
If something is on its way, it will arrive soon.

‡‡ **pretend** [priténd] v. ~인 척하다, ~인 것처럼 굴다; ~라고 가장하다
If you pretend that something is the case, you act in a way that is intended to make people believe that it is the case, although in fact it is not.

★ **litter** [lítər] n. 쓰레기; v. 어지럽히다; (쓰레기 등을) 버리다
Litter is rubbish that is left lying around outside.

hallway [hɔ́lwèi] n. 복도; 통로
A hallway in a building is a long passage with doors into rooms on both sides of it.

⁑ **evil** [íːvəl] a. 사악한, 악랄한; 유해한; 악마의; n. 악
If you describe someone or something is evil, you mean that they are morally bad and causing great harm, especially to society in general.

⋆ **itch** [itʃ] v. 가렵다, 가렵게 하다; n. 가려움
When a part of your body itches, you have an unpleasant feeling on your skin that makes you want to scratch.

⋆ **scratch** [skrætʃ] v. 긁다; 긁힌 자국을 내다; n. 긁힌 자국; 긁는 소리
If you scratch yourself, you rub your fingernails against your skin because it is itching.

복습 **outlet** [áutlet] n. 콘센트; (액체·기체의) 배출구
An outlet is a place, usually in a wall, where you can connect electrical devices to the electricity supply.

복습 **short** [ʃɔːrt] v. (전기 회로 등을) 합선시키다; a. 짧은; 부족한
If an electrical device is shorted out, a wrong connection or damaged wire causes electricity to travel along the wrong route and damage the device.

⋆ **dumb** [dʌm] a. 멍청한, 바보 같은; 말을 못 하는
If you call a person dumb, you mean that they are stupid or foolish.

복습 **exact** [igzǽkt] a. 정확한; 꼼꼼한, 빈틈없는; 바로 그 (exactly ad. 정확히)
You use exactly to emphasize that something is correct in every way or in every detail.

⋆ **genius** [dʒíːnjəs] n. 천재; 천재성; 특별한 재능
A genius is a highly talented, creative, or intelligent person.

keyhole [kíːhòul] n. 열쇠 구멍
A keyhole is the hole in a lock that you put a key in.

★ peer [piər] v. 자세히 들여다보다, 주의해서 보다
If you peer at something, you look at it very hard, usually because it is difficult to see clearly.

‡ swing [swiŋ] v. (swung-swung) 휙 움직이다; 휘두르다; (전후·좌우로) 흔들다 n. 흔들기
If something swings in a particular direction or if you swing it in that direction, it moves in that direction with a smooth, curving movement.

★ scramble [skræmbl] v. 재빨리 움직이다; 간신히 해내다
(scramble to one's feet idiom 허둥지둥 일어나다)
If you scramble to a different place or position, you move there in a hurried, awkward way.

‡ trip [trip] v. 걸려 넘어지다, 발을 헛디디다; 넘어뜨리다; n. 여행
If you trip when you are walking, you knock your foot against something and fall or nearly fall.

fall flat on one's face idiom 앞으로 넘어지다; 실패하다
If you fall flat on your face, you fall forward so that you are lying on your front.

★ giant [dʒáiənt] n. 거인; a. 거대한, 위대한
A giant is an imaginary person who is very big and strong, especially one mentioned in old stories.

rumble [rʌmbl] v. 우르릉거리는 소리를 내다; n. 우르렁거리는 소리
If something rumbles, it makes a low, continuous noise.

★ slap [slæp] v. (손바닥으로) 철썩 때리다; 털썩 놓다; n. 철썩 때리기, 치기
If you slap someone or something, you hit them with the palm of your hand.

★ dust [dʌst] n. 먼지, 티끌; 흙먼지; v. 먼지를 털다; (고운 가루를) 뿌리다
Dust is the very small pieces of dirt which you find inside buildings, for example on furniture, floors, or lights.

‡ demand [dimǽnd] v. 강력히 묻다, 따지다; 요구하다; n. 요구; 수요
If you demand something, you ask a question in a very firm or angry way.

^{복습}**fasten** [fæsn] v. (시선을 오랫동안) 고정시키다; 매다, 채우다; (단단히) 잠그다
If your eyes fasten on someone or something, you look at them for a long time.

*＊**lean** [li:n] v. (몸을) 숙이다, 기울이다; ~에 기대다; a. 군살이 없는, 호리호리한
When you lean in a particular direction, you bend your body in that direction.

way [wei] ad. 훨씬; 아주 멀리; n. 방법; 길
You can use way to emphasize, for example, that something is a great distance away or is very much below or above a particular level or amount.

^{복습}**scare** [skɛər] v. 무서워하다; 놀라게 하다; n. 불안(감); 놀람, 공포 (scared a. 무서워하는)
If you are scared, you are frightened of something or afraid that something bad might happen.

*＊**hammer** [hǽmər] n. 망치, 해머; v. 망치로 치다; 쿵쿵 치다
A hammer is a tool with a handle and a heavy metal head, used for breaking things or hitting nails.

clonk [klɑŋk] v. (쾅) 치다; 쾅 하는 소리를 내다; n. 쾅 하는 소리
To clonk means to hit something, making a short loud sound.

*＊**sight** [sait] n. 광경, 모습; 보기, 봄; 시야; v. 갑자기 보다
A sight is something that you see.

^{복습}**tune** [tju:n] v. (채널을) 맞추다; 음을 맞추다; n. 곡, 선율; (마음의) 상태
To tune in to something or tune in on something means to watch or listen to a particular television or radio program or station.

give a break idiom 그만 좀 해!; ~를 너그럽게 봐주다
You can say 'give me a break' to show that you are annoyed by what someone has said or done.

*＊**expect** [ikspékt] v. 예상하다, 기대하다
If you expect something to happen, you believe that it will happen.

‡kill [kil] v. 몹시 웃게 하다; 죽이다

If you say that someone or something kills you, you mean that they make you laugh a lot.

＊puzzle [pʌzl] v. 어리둥절하게 하다; n. 퍼즐; 수수께끼 (puzzled a. 어리둥절해하는)

Someone who is puzzled is confused because they do not understand something.

cross off idiom (명단에 선을 그어서) 지우다, 빼다

If you cross off words on a list, you decide that they no longer belong on the list, and often you draw a line through them to indicate this.

‡list [list] n. 명단, 목록; v. (특정한 순서로) 열거하다

A list of things such as names or addresses is a set of them which all belong to a particular category, written down one below the other.

Chapter 7

1. **What did Mrs. Coleman-Levin want Zack to do?**

   A. Have science class by himself

   B. Skip his other morning classes

   C. Eat lunch in the classroom

   D. Talk to her alone after lunch

2. **What was weird about Zack's phone call to his dad?**

   A. His dad refused to pick up Zack at school.

   B. His dad did not answer the phone.

   C. His dad pretended he was busy.

   D. His dad hesitated to tell Zack where he was.

3. What did Zack do before he went back to his classroom?

   A. He told the nurse he was not feeling well.

   B. He hid under Spencer's table at lunch.

   C. He stayed behind longer in his other classes.

   D. He ate his food very slowly.

4. What kind of plan did Zack have for dealing with Mrs. Coleman-Levin?

   A. A detailed plan that involved trapping her

   B. A crazy plan that involved throwing things

   C. A smart plan that involved kicking

   D. A basic plan that involved running away

5. Why did the lights turn off in the classroom?

   A. Someone hit the light switch.

   B. Someone removed the light bulbs.

   C. The storm cut off the power to the lights.

   D. Thunder made the lights fall down and break.

Check Your Reading Speed

1분에 몇 단어를 읽는지 리딩 속도를 측정해보세요.

$$\frac{578 \text{ words}}{\text{reading time (} \qquad \text{) sec}} \times 60 = (\qquad) \text{ WPM}$$

Build Your Vocabulary

✱ **fling** [fliŋ] v. 내던지다; (힘껏) 던지다; (욕설 등을) 퍼붓다; n. 내던지기
If you fling something somewhere, you throw it there using a lot of force.

⁎ **lightning** [láitniŋ] n. 번개, 번갯불; a. 아주 빠른; 급작스러운
Lightning is the very bright flashes of light in the sky that happen during thunderstorms.

✱ **flash** [flæʃ] v. (잠깐) 번쩍이다, 비치다; 휙 움직이다; n. 섬광, 번쩍임
If a light flashes, it shines brightly for a very short time, or shines on and off very quickly.

복습 **thunder** [θʌ́ndər] n. 천둥; 천둥 같은 소리; v. 천둥이 치다; 우르릉거리다
Thunder is the loud noise that you hear from the sky after a flash of lightning, especially during a storm.

✱ **crash** [kræʃ] v. 굉음을 내다; 충돌하다; n. 요란한 소리; (자동차·항공기) 사고
If something crashes, it makes a sudden loud noise.

⁎ **attendance** [əténdəns] n. 출석, 참석 (take attendance idiom 출석을 확인하다)
If you take attendance, you check who is present and who is not present at a place and mark this information on a list of names.

crave [kreiv] v. 열망하다, 갈망하다; 간절히 청하다
If you crave something, you want to have it very much.

taste [teist] n. 맛; 취향; 감식력, 감각; v. 맛이 나다
The taste of something is the flavor that something creates in your mouth when you eat or drink it.

blood [blʌd] n. 피, 혈액
Blood is the red liquid that flows inside your body, which you can see if you cut yourself.

yikes [jaiks] int. 이크, 으악 (놀랐을 때 내는 소리)
Yikes is used to show that you are worried, surprised, or shocked.

expression [ikspréʃən] n. 표정; 표현, 어구
Your expression is a look on your face that shows what your thought or feeling is.

stutter [stʌ́tər] v. 말을 더듬다, 더듬거리다; n. 말을 더듬기
When you stutter, you repeat the sounds of words in an uncontrolled way when you speak because you are nervous or have a speech problem.

squeak [skwiːk] n. 찍 하는 소리; v. 꽥 소리치다; 끽 하는 소리를 내다
A squeak is a short, high cry or sound.

swallow [swálou] v. (초조해서) 마른침을 삼키다; 집어삼키다; n. 삼키기; [동물] 제비
If you swallow, you make a movement in your throat as if you are moving something from your mouth into your stomach, because you are nervous or frightened.

psycho [sáikou] n. (아주 이상하게 폭력적인) 정신병자; a. 정신병의; 정신 의학의
A psycho is someone who has serious mental problems and who may act in a violent way without feeling sorry for what they have done.

victim [víktim] n. (범죄·질병·사고 등의) 피해자
A victim is someone who has been harmed, injured, or killed as the result of a crime.

geography [dʒiágrəfi] n. 지리학; (한 지역의) 지리, 지형
Geography is the study of the countries of the world and of such things as the land, seas, climate, towns, and population.

^{복습} **weird** [wiərd] a. 기이한, 기묘한; 기괴한, 섬뜩한
If you describe something or someone as weird, you mean that they are strange.

[☆] **temperature** [témpərəʧər] n. 체온, (몸의) 열; 온도, 기온
Your temperature is the degree of internal heat of your body, especially used as a measure of whether you are sick or not.

amusement park [əmjú:zmənt pa:rk] n. 놀이공원
An amusement park is a large park with many special machines that you can ride on or play games to win prizes.

^{☆☆} **alive** [əláiv] a. 살아 있는; (생기·감정 등이) 넘치는
If people or animals are alive, they are not dead.

^{복습} **storm** [stɔ:rm] n. 폭풍, 폭풍우; v. 기습하다; 쿵쾅대며 가다
A storm is very bad weather, with heavy rain, strong winds, and often thunder and lightning.

[☆] **upstairs** [ʌpstéərz] ad. 위층으로; 위층에; n. 위층
If you go upstairs in a building, you go up a staircase toward a higher floor.

^{☆☆} **pull** [pul] v. (범죄 등을) 저지르다; 끌다; n. 끌기
If you pull something, you succeed in doing something illegal or dishonest or in playing a trick on someone.

^{복습} **funny** [fʌ́ni] a. 수상쩍은, 의심스러운; 이상한; 웃기는
If you describe something as funny, you think it is strange, surprising, or puzzling.

[★] **scream** [skri:m] v. 비명을 지르다; 소리치다; n. 비명, 절규
When someone screams, they make a very loud, high-pitched cry, because they are in pain or are very frightened.

run for one's life idiom (필사적으로) 도망치다; 간신히 도망가다
If you run for your life, you run away to escape from great danger.

pressure [préʃər] n. 압박감; 압력; v. 압력을 가하다
(under pressure idiom 압박감을 느끼는)
If you are under pressure, you feel that you must do a lot of tasks or make a lot of decisions in very little time, or that people expect a lot from you.

creepy [kríːpi] a. 기분 나쁜, 오싹한
If you say that someone or something is creepy, you mean they are strange or unnatural, making you feel frightened.

skeleton [skélətn] n. 해골; 뼈대, 골격; (건물 등의) 골격
Skeleton is the set of bones that supports a human or animal body, or a model of this.

grin [grin] v. (소리 없이) 활짝 웃다; n. 활짝 웃음
When you grin, you smile broadly.

clap [klæp] n. 쿵 하는 소리; 박수; v. 박수를 치다; 쾅하고 놓다
A clap of thunder is a sudden and loud noise of thunder.

go out idiom (불·전깃불이) 꺼지다; 외출하다
If the fire or the light goes out, it stops burning or shining.

knock out idiom ~을 쓸 수 없게 하다; 기절시키다
To knock out means to destroy something, or to stop it working.

freak [friːk] v. 기겁하게 하다; 기겁하다; n. 괴짜 (freak out idiom 기겁하게 하다)
If you are freaked out or if something freaks you out, you become so angry, surprised, excited, or frightened that you cannot control yourself.

halfway [hǽfwèi] ad. (거리·시간상으로) 중간에, 가운데쯤에; 꽤 괜찮은
Halfway means in the middle of a place or between two points, at an equal distance from each of them.

pick up idiom (어떤 정보를) 알게 되다; ~을 집어 올리다, 줍다
If you pick up interesting or useful information, you learn it from someone or something.

Chapter 8

1. What happened when the lights came back on?

A. Zack saw a shadow next to him.

B. Zack did not see anyone in the classroom.

C. Zack felt like someone was behind him.

D. Zack did not feel like anything was wrong anymore.

2. What did Zack think when he heard the killer's thoughts again?

A. It was odd that the killer had not killed him yet.

B. It no longer sounded like the killer wanted to hurt him.

C. It would not be possible for the killer to swallow him.

D. It did not make sense that the killer would attack him at school.

3. What did Zack do when he saw the little fish and the piranha?

A. He moved the little fish to another tank.

B. He scooped up the piranha with a fishnet.

C. He pushed the little fish to the corner of the tank.

D. He slapped the piranha with his hand.

4. How did the little fish feel after Zack saved it?

A. It felt tough and brave.

B. It felt guilty and ashamed.

C. It felt confused and scared.

D. It felt lucky and thankful.

5. Why did Zack pick up the electric cord?

A. To throw it in the trash can

B. To distract the piranha with it

C. To create sparks with it

D. To reconnect it with the motor

Check Your Reading Speed
1분에 몇 단어를 읽는지 리딩 속도를 측정해보세요.

$$\frac{392 \text{ words}}{\text{reading time ( ) sec}} \times 60 = (\qquad) \text{ WPM}$$

Build Your Vocabulary

scream [skri:m] v. 비명을 지르다; 소리치다; n. 비명, 절규
When someone screams, they make a very loud, high-pitched cry, because they are in pain or are very frightened.

rush [rʌʃ] v. 급히 움직이다; 서두르다; n. (감정이 갑자기) 치밀어 오름; 혼잡
If you rush somewhere, you go there quickly.

★ unfortunate [ʌnfɔ́:rʧənət] a. 유감스러운; 불운한 (unfortunately ad. 불행하게도)
You can use unfortunately to introduce or refer to a statement when you consider that it is sad or disappointing, or when you want to express regret.

trip [trip] v. 걸려 넘어지다, 발을 헛디디다; 넘어뜨리다; n. 여행
If you trip when you are walking, you knock your foot against something and fall or nearly fall.

shoot [ʃu:t] v. (shot-shot) 찌릿하다; 분출하다; 발사하다; int. 말해라
If pain shoots through your body, you feel it going quickly through it.

‡ knee [ni:] n. 무릎; v. 무릎으로 치다
Your knee is the place where your leg bends.

thunder [θʌ́ndər] n. 천둥; 천둥 같은 소리; v. 천둥이 치다; 우르릉거리다
Thunder is the loud noise that you hear from the sky after a flash of lightning, especially during a storm.

explode [iksplóud] v. 굉음을 내다; 폭발하다; (강한 감정을) 터뜨리다
If something explodes, it makes a sudden very loud noise.

admit [ædmít] v. 인정하다, 시인하다; 들어가게 하다
If you admit that something bad, unpleasant, or embarrassing is true, you agree, often unwillingly, that it is true.

kid [kid] v. 스스로를 속이다, 착각하다; 농담하다; n. 아이
If people kid themselves, they allow themselves to believe something that is not true because they wish that it was true.

flicker [flíkər] v. (불·빛 등이) 깜박거리다; 움직거리다; n. (빛의) 깜박거림; 움직거림
If a flame or light flickers, it does not burn evenly, or it goes on and off.

blink [bliŋk] v. 눈을 깜박이다; (불빛이) 깜박거리다; n. 눈을 깜박거림
When you blink or when you blink your eyes, you shut your eyes and very quickly open them again.

glare [glɛər] n. 환한 빛, 눈부심; 노려봄; v. 환하다, 눈부시다; 노려보다
Glare is very bright light that is difficult to look at.

soul [soul] n. 사람; 영혼; 마음; 정신
You use soul in negative statements like not a soul to mean nobody at all.

figure out idiom ~을 이해하다, 알아내다; 계산하다, 산출하다
If you figure out a solution to a problem or the reason for something, you succeed in solving it or understanding it.

trap [træp] v. (위험한 장소·궁지에) 가두다; 함정에 빠뜨리다; n. 덫; 함정
To trap someone or something means to force them into a place or situation that they cannot escape from, especially in order to catch them.

swallow [swálou] v. 집어삼키다; (초조해서) 마른침을 삼키다; n. 삼키기; [동물] 제비
If you swallow something, you cause it to go from your mouth down into your stomach.

out of the corner of one's eye idiom 곁눈질로; 흘낏 보고
If you see something out of the corner of your eye, you see it but not clearly because it happens to the side of you.

motion [móuʃən] n. 움직임; 동작, 몸짓; v. (손·머리로) 몸짓을 해 보이다
A motion is a movement that someone or something makes.

tank [tæŋk] n. 수조; (액체·가스를 담는) 탱크; 전차, 탱크
A tank is a large glass container for animals such as fish or snakes.

be about to idiom 막 ~하려는 참이다
If you are about to do something, you are going to do it immediately.

receive [risíːv] v. (무선을) 듣다; 수신하다; 받다, 받아들이다
To receive means to be able to hear someone's voice when they are communicating with you by radio.

spring [spriŋ] v. (sprang-sprung) 뛰어오르다; 튀다; n. 샘; 봄; 생기, 활기
When a person or animal springs, they jump upward or forward suddenly or quickly.

jaw [dʒɔː] n. 턱
Your jaw is the lower part of your face below your mouth.

gulp [gʌlp] v. 꿀꺽꿀꺽 삼키다; (공포·놀라움에) 침을 꿀떡 삼키다; n. 꿀꺽 마시기
If you gulp something, you eat or drink it very quickly by swallowing large quantities of it at once.

slap [slæp] v. (손바닥으로) 철썩 때리다; 털썩 놓다; n. 철썩 때리기, 치기
If you slap someone or something, you hit them with the palm of your hand.

fishnet [fíʃnet] n. 어망, 그물
A fishnet is a net for catching fish.

scoop [skuːp] v. (큰 숟갈 같은 것으로) 뜨다; 재빨리 들어 올리다; n. 국자; 한 숟갈
If you scoop something, you dig something out or pick it up using something such as a spoon or your curved hand.

plop [plap] v. 퐁당 넣다; 털썩 주저앉다; n. 퐁당 하는 소리
If you plop something, you drop it into a liquid, so that it makes a short, soft sound.

★ splash [splæʃ] v. (물 등을) 튀기다, 끼얹다; 첨벙거리다; n. 첨벙 하는 소리
If you splash a liquid somewhere or if it splashes, it hits someone or something and scatters in a lot of small drops.

teeny [tíːni] a. 아주 작은
If you describe something as teeny, you are emphasizing that it is very small.

★ miracle [mírəkl] n. 기적; 기적 같은 일
A miracle is a wonderful and surprising event that is believed to be caused by God.

⁂ loose [luːs] a. 풀린; 헐거워진; 느슨한; v. 느슨하게 하다, 풀다
Something that is loose is not firmly held or fixed in place.

복습 electric [iléktrik] a. 전기의; 전기를 이용하는
An electric device or machine works by means of electricity, rather than using some other source of power.

★ cord [kɔːrd] n. 전선; 끈, 줄
Cord is wire covered in rubber or plastic which connects electrical equipment to an electricity supply.

★ filter [fíltər] n. 여과 장치; v. 여과하다, 거르다; 새어 들어오다
A filter is an object or piece of equipment that allows you to remove solid parts that are not wanted from a liquid or gas.

복습 motor [móutər] n. 모터, 전동기; a. 모터가 달린
The motor in a machine, vehicle, or boat is the part that uses electricity or fuel to produce movement, so that the machine, vehicle, or boat can work.

aquarium [əkwéəriəm] n. 수조; 수족관
An aquarium is a glass tank filled with water, in which people keep fish.

yank [jæŋk] v. 휙 잡아당기다; n. 휙 잡아당기기
If you yank someone or something somewhere, you pull them there suddenly and with a lot of force.

★ **distract** [distrǽkt] v. (주의를) 딴 데로 돌리다, 집중이 안 되게 하다
If something distracts you or your attention from something, it takes your attention away from it.

⚡ **bend** [bend] v. (bent-bent) (몸·머리를) 숙이다; 구부리다; n. (도로·강의) 굽이, 굽은 곳
When you bend, you move the top part of your body downward and forward.

★ **plug** [plʌg] v. 밀어넣다, 꽂다; n. (전기) 플러그; 마개
If you plug something into something else, you connect a piece of equipment to an electricity supply or to another piece of equipment.

⚡ **wet** [wet] a. 젖은, 축축한
If something is wet, it is covered in water, rain, sweat, tears, or another liquid.

복습 **flash** [flæʃ] n. 섬광, 번쩍임; v. (잠깐) 번쩍이다, 비치다; 휙 움직이다
A flash is a sudden burst of light or of something shiny or bright.

복습 **tingle** [tiŋgl] v. 따끔거리다, 얼얼하다; (어떤 감정이) 마구 일다; n. 따끔거림; 흥분
When a part of your body tingles, you have a slight stinging feeling there.

firecracker [fáiərkrækər] n. 폭죽
A firecracker is a firework that makes several loud bangs when it is lit.

복습 **go off** idiom 터지다, 폭발하다; (경보기 등이) 울리다
If an explosive device or a gun goes off, it explodes or fires.

복습 **black out** idiom (일시적으로) 의식을 잃다
If you black out, you become unconscious or lose your memory for a short time.

Chapter 9

1. **What was the reaction when Zack woke up?**

   A. Everyone was eager to let him go home and rest.

   B. Zack's dad was sorry for not arriving sooner.

   C. Mrs. Coleman-Levin was glad he was all right.

   D. Mrs. Krump was embarrassed that he had injured himself again.

2. **What was Mrs. Coleman-Levin's surprise?**

   A. Zack was going to name a new class pet.

   B. Zack was going to look after a class pet.

   C. Zack was going to have a long vacation.

   D. Zack was going to spend his vacation at school.

3. Why couldn't Zack read people's thoughts anymore?

   A. Mind-reading powers lasted only a few days.

   B. Mind-reading powers required a lot of energy.

   C. Getting electrocuted again made him lose the ability.

   D. Getting shocked a second time made him too weak.

4. What did Zack's dad assume at first?

   A. Zack could teach everyone how to read minds.

   B. Zack had no desire to read minds anymore.

   C. Zack never actually had the power to read minds.

   D. Zack still had the power to read minds.

5. How did Zack feel about losing his mind-reading powers?

   A. He was pretty much fine with it.

   B. He really missed being special.

   C. He wished he had appreciated his powers more.

   D. He felt like the luckiest person in the world.

Check Your Reading Speed
1분에 몇 단어를 읽는지 리딩 속도를 측정해보세요.

$$\frac{499 \ words}{reading \ time \ (\quad) \ sec} \times 60 = (\quad) \ WPM$$

Build Your Vocabulary

cot [kat] n. 병원 침대; 야영용 간이 침대; 아기 침대
A cot is a narrow bed, usually made of canvas fitted over a frame which can be folded up.

복습 **stare** [stɛər] v. 빤히 쳐다보다, 응시하다; n. 빤히 쳐다보기, 응시
If you stare at someone or something, you look at them for a long time.

not so hot idiom (몸·기분이) 별로 좋지 못한
If you feel not so hot, you are not feeling very well or very happy.

복습 **scare** [skɛər] n. 놀람, 공포; 불안(감); v. 무서워하다; 놀라게 하다
If a sudden unpleasant experience gives you a scare, it frightens you.

복습 **dumb** [dʌm] a. 멍청한, 바보 같은; 말을 못 하는
If you call a person dumb, you mean that they are stupid or foolish.

복습 **electrocute** [iléktrəkjùːt] v. 감전 사고를 입히다; 감전사시키다
If someone is electrocuted, they are accidentally killed or badly injured when they touch something connected to a source of electricity.

복습 **manage** [mǽnidʒ] v. 간신히 해내다; 운영하다, 관리하다; 처리하다
If you say that someone managed a particular response, such as a laugh or a greeting, you mean that it was difficult for them to do it because they were feeling sad or upset.

homeroom [hóumrum] n. 생활 학급
In a school, homeroom is the class or room where students in the same grade meet to get general information and be checked for attendance.

psycho [sáikou] n. (아주 이상하게 폭력적인) 정신병자; a. 정신병의; 정신 의학의
A psycho is someone who has serious mental problems and who may act in a violent way without feeling sorry for what they have done.

after all idiom 결국에는; 어쨌든
You use after all when you are saying that something that you thought might not be the case is in fact the case.

take care of idiom ~을 돌보다; ~을 처리하다
To take care of means to protect someone or something and provide the things that that person or thing needs.

murder [mə́:rdər] v. 살해하다, 살인하다; n. 살해, 살인죄 (murderer n. 살인자)
A murderer is someone who illegally and intentionally killed another person.

pat [pæt] v. 쓰다듬다, 토닥거리다; n. 쓰다듬기, 토닥거리기
If you pat something or someone, you tap them lightly, usually with your hand held flat.

hit [hit] v. (hit-hit) (생각 등이 불현듯) 떠오르다; 부딪치다; 치다; n. 치기
When a feeling or an idea hits you, it suddenly affects you or comes into your mind.

knock out idiom ~을 쓸 수 없게 하다; 기절시키다
To knock out means to destroy something, or to stop it working.

check out idiom ~을 확인하다; 살펴보다
If you check out something or someone, you find out information about them to make sure that everything is correct or satisfactory.

amaze [əméiz] v. (대단히) 놀라게 하다; 경악하게 하다 (amazing a. 놀라운)
You say that something is amazing when it is very surprising and makes you feel pleasure, approval, or wonder.

★ **absolute** [ǽbsəlùːt] a. 완전한, 완벽한; 확실한 (absolutely ad. 틀림없이)
Absolutely means totally and completely.

복습 **frown** [fraun] v. 얼굴을 찡그리다; 눈살을 찌푸리다; n. 찡그림, 찌푸림
When someone frowns, their eyebrows become drawn together, because they are annoyed or puzzled.

복습 **puzzle** [pʌzl] v. 어리둥절하게 하다; n. 퍼즐; 수수께끼 (puzzlement n. 어리둥절함)
Puzzlement is the confusion that you feel when you do not understand something.

★ **embarrass** [imbǽrəs] v. 당황스럽게 하다, 어색하게 하다; 곤란하게 하다
(embarrassed a. 당황스러운)
If you feel embarrassed, you are ashamed of something and worried about what other people will think of you.

복습 **nod** [nad] v. (고개를) 끄덕이다, 까딱하다; n. 끄덕임
If you nod, you move your head downward and upward to show that you are answering 'yes' to a question, or to show agreement, understanding, or approval.

복습 **pick up** idiom (어떤 정보를) 알게 되다; ~을 집어 올리다, 줍다
If you pick up interesting or useful information, you learn it from someone or something.

★ **complicate** [kámpləkèit] v. 복잡하게 하다; 복잡해지다
To complicate something means to make it more difficult to understand or deal with.

1장

사람들의 마음을 읽을 수 있었으면 좋겠다고 바란 적이 있나요? 사람들의 머릿속에 채널을 맞추고 무슨 생각을 하고 있는지 그대로 듣는 것이요? 흠, 잊어버리세요. 그게 별로 마음에 들지 않을 거예요. 제가 알아요. 저는 그걸 해봤거든요. 그리고 그건 그리 즐거운 일이 아니었어요. 정말이에요.

제가 처음부터 이야기를 시작해야 할 것 같네요. 제 이름은 잭(Zack)입니다. 열 살이고요. 뉴욕시(New York City)에 살아요. 그리고 저는 호러스 하이드-화이트 남학교(Horace Hyde-White School for Boys) 5학년입니다.

제가 어렸을 때부터, 저는 기이한 일에 관심을 가져 왔습니다. 저는 저 자신이 이상하다고는 생각하지 않습니다. 그렇지만 외계인들이 저를 그들의 우주선으로 초대해 줬으면 좋겠다고 계속 바라고 있기는 합니다. 아니면 영혼이 몸에서 빠져나가 둥실둥실 떠다니면서 주유소 화장실에 들르지 않고도 멀리 여행할 수 있었으면 좋겠다고 바라기도 하지요. 주유소 화장실은 언제나 아주 역겨우니까요.

과학이 아마 제가 제일 좋아하는 과목일 것입니다. 그것은 적어도 마음을 읽는 것 만큼 이상한 것을 가르쳐 줍니다. 예를 들면, 타키온(tachyon)이 무엇인지 알고 있나요? 타키온은 세상에서 가장 작은 것 중 하나입니다. 심지어, 원자보다도 더 작습니다. 그리고 그것은 빛의 속도보다 더 빠르게 이동합니다. 타키온은 너무 빨리 이동해서, 출발하기도 전에 가려던 곳에 도착해 있습니다. 만약 여러분이 타키온이라면, 여러분은 절대 학교에 지각하지 않을 겁니다. 집을 떠나기도 전에 거기 도착해 있겠죠. 저는 그것을 과학 수업에서 배웠습니다.

제가 여러분에게 말하고 싶은 순간은 과학 시간에 일어났습니다. 콜먼-레빈 선생님(Mrs. Coleman-Levin)이 제 과학 선생님입니다. 그녀는 제 담임 선생님이기도 합니다. 그녀는 좀 기이한 편인데, 나쁜 쪽으로 그렇다는 것은 아닙니다. 우선, 그녀는 언제나 작업용 부츠를 신고 있습니다. 여름에도 말입니다. 심지어 저녁에 학교에서 열리는 잘 차려입어야 하는 파티에서도요. 또 한 가지, 그녀는 주말에 시체 안치소에서 일합니다. 그녀는 부검을 합니다. 그러니까 죽은 사람을 조각조각 잘라서 그들이 무엇 때문에 죽었는지 확인한다는 뜻입니다. 징그럽죠. 하지만 흥미롭습니다.

우리 교실에는 이상하고, 재미있는 것이 많이 있습니다. 구석에는 사람 해골이 통째로 걸려 있습니다. 게다가, 플라스틱 모형도 아닙니다. 그것은 진짜 해골입니다. 자신의 책상 위에, 콜먼-레빈 선생님은 돼지 뇌가 들어 있는 유리병을 놓아 둡니다. 그리고 우리는 학급 애완동물도 많이 가지고 있습니다. 하지만 귀엽고, 털이 북슬북슬한 종류는 아닙니다. 우리는 피라냐 물고기(piranha fish)와 타란툴라(tarantula) 그리고 뱀을 가지고 있습니다. 피라냐는 금붕어를 먹습니다. 뱀은 쥐를 먹는데, 좀 징그럽죠. 콜먼-레빈 선생님은 우리가 주변에 없을 때 그것들에게 먹이를 줍니다. 그녀는 그것에 전혀 개의치않는 것 같습니다.

제가 여러분에게 이야기하고 싶은 그날, 콜먼-레빈 선생님은 우리가 실험하는 것을 도와주고 있었습니다. 실험은 작은 전기 모터를 가지고 하는 것이었습니다. 저는 전기 모터를 연결하고 있었습니다. 우연히, 전선 하나가 물이 담긴 비커(beaker) 안으로 떨어졌습니다. 별 생각 없이, 저는 손을 넣어서 그것을 꺼냈습니다. 갑자기 제 손이 온통 따끔거렸습니다. 마치 전기 스파크가 제 몸에서 발사되는 것처럼 느껴졌습니다.

"잭!" 콜먼-레빈 선생님이 저를 향해 달려왔습니다. "너 괜찮니?"

"어, 그럼요. 어느 정도는요." 제가 말했습니다.

진실을 알고 싶다면, 저는 그때 제가 정말 괜찮은지 알 수 없었습니다. 저는 작은 불꽃들이 터지는 것을 지켜보느라 너무 정신이 없었거든요—펑! 펑!—제 눈 바로 앞에서 말입니다. 그 후 저는 완전히 의식을 잃었습니다.

2장

"좀 어떠니, 애야?" 낯설고, 메아리치는 목소리가 말했습니다.

양호 교사, 크럼프 선생님(Mrs. Krump)이었습니다. 그녀의 목소리는 평소에는 울리지 않습니다.

"괜찮아요, 감사합니다." 저는 말했습니다. 제가 괜찮지 않을 때도, 저는 언제나 "괜찮아요, 감사합니다"라고 대답합니다. 사람들이 안부를 물어볼 때, 실제로 알고 싶은 게 아니란 것을 저는 알게 되었습니다. 그들은 그저 여러분이 괜찮다고 말해서 다음 주제로 넘어갈 수 있기를 원할 뿐입니다.

"그런데요." 제가 말했습니다. "제가 왜 여기에 있나요?"

"너 기억 안 나니?" 크럼프 선생님이 그녀의 메아리치는 목소리로 말했습니다.

"기억나죠. 어느 정도는요." 제가 말했습니다. "하지만 그래도 말해 주세요."

"음, 너는 과학 수업 시간에 감전되었어." 그녀가 말했습니다. "전기가 흐르는 전선이 있는 물이 담긴 비커에 네가 손을 넣었어. 그게 너를 기절시켰단다."

"아, 맞아요." 제가 말했습니다. "저도 기억나요."

그리고 그때 이상한 일이 일어났습니다. 그녀의 입술이 움직이지 않았는데도, 크럼프 선생님이 말하는 것을 들은 것 같았습니다, 멍청한 얼뜨기 같으니라고. 네가 감전돼서 죽지 않은 게 천만다행이다.

"뭐라고 하셨어요?" 제가 말했습니다.

"뭐?" 크럼프 선생님이 말했습니다.

"선생님이 방금 저를 멍청한 얼뜨기라고 부르셨잖아요."

크럼프 선생님의 얼굴이 새빨개졌습니다.

"나는 그런 말은 하지 않았어." 그녀가 대답했습니다. 그리고 나서, 그녀의 입술이 전혀 움직이지 않았는데도, 저는 그녀가 말하는 것을 들었습니다, 작은 소리로 중얼거리고 있었나 보네. 조심해야겠어.

그녀가 그것을 어떻게 했는지 모르겠습니다. 아마도 그녀는 복화술사인가 봅니다.

"그거 어떻게 하셨어요?" 제가 물었습니다.

"내가 뭘 어떻게 했다는 말이니?"

"입술을 움직이지 않고 방금 그렇게 말하는 것 말이에요."

크럼프 선생님은 얼굴을 찡그렸습니다. 그녀는 저를 의심스럽다는 듯이 보았습니다. 그녀는 저를 15분 동안 누워 있게 했습니다. 그녀는 제 입에 체온계를 찔러 넣었습니다. 그러더니 그녀는 말했습니다. "잭, 너 열은 없구나. 그리고 심하게 다친 것처럼 보이지도 않고. 다음 수업을 들으러 가겠니?"

"그럴게요." 제가 말했습니다.

만약 다음 수업이 무엇이었는지 제가 기억하고 있었다면, 저는 아마 그러겠다고 대답하지 않았을 것입니다.

3장

다음 수업은 지리였습니다. 저는 지리를 굉장히 좋아합니다. 하지만 우리는 그날 아주 중요한 시험이 있었습니다. 그리고 저는 공부하기 위해 지리책을 집으로 가져가는 것을 잊어버렸습니다. 그러니까 저는 망했죠.

우리 지리 선생님, 스노드그라스 선생님(Mr. Snodgrass)이, 시험 문제가 있는 종이를 나눠주었습니다. 저는 제 시험지를 살펴보았고 어지러워지기 시작했습니다. 첫 번째 문제는, "이라크(Iraq)에서 가장 큰 강의 이름을 두 개

쓰시오."였습니다.

심장이 돌덩이처럼 가라앉았습니다. 저는 아는 것이 전혀 없었습니다. 이라크가 어느 대륙에 있는지도 확실하지 않았습니다. 그때 갑자기 제 머릿속에 어떤 모습이 팍 들어왔습니다. 저는 그것이 어디에서 왔는지 몰랐습니다. 어미 호랑이가 새끼 호랑이들과 함께 있는 모습이었습니다. 그리고 가까이에는 한 무리의 아이들이 있었는데, 겁에 질린 것처럼 보였습니다. 새끼 호랑이들은 계속해서, "이 겁쟁이들(You Fraidies)!"이라고 아이들에게 소리쳤습니다.

도대체 그게 이라크에 있는 강들과 무슨 상관이 있는 거죠?

그때 저는 제 머릿속에서 어떤 목소리를 들었습니다. 암컷 호랑이(Tigress)와 이 겁쟁이들(you Fraidies), 그 목소리가 말했습니다. 바로 그거였어요! 이라크에서 가장 큰 강 두 개는 티그리스강(Tigris)과 유프라테스강(Euphrates)이었어요! 하지만 제가 어떻게 그것을 기억해 냈을까요? 저는 재빨리 정답을 적었습니다.

저는 두 번째 문제를 살펴봤습니다. "세계에서 가장 높은 산은 무엇인가?" 저는 그 문제를 건너뛰려고 했습니다. 하지만 그때 또다시 제 머릿속에 정답이 팍 떠올랐습니다. 조금 전처럼 말입니다. 에베레스트산(Mount Everest).

와! 저는 정말 기뻤습니다. 저는 제가 생각했던 것보다 더 많이 알고 있었습니다!

저는 계속해서 다음 질문으로 넘어갔습니다. "세계의 대륙들을 크기순으로 나열하시오." 오, 맙소사. 제가 똑똑하다는 생각이 이제는 들지 않았습니다. 저는 아시아(Asia)가 끝내주게 크다는 것은 알고 있었습니다. 그리고 북아메리카(North America)와 남아메리카(South America)가 대륙이라는 것도 알고 있었고요. 그런데 오스트레일리아(Australia)는 대륙이었던가요, 아니면 아주 커다란 섬이었던가요? 그리고...

저는 더 생각할 필요가 없었습니다. 제 머릿속의 목소리가 말했습니다, 어디 보자... 아시아, 아프리카(Africa), 북아메리카, 남아메리카, 남극 대륙(Antarctica), 유럽(Europe), 그리고 오스트레일—

바로 그때 저는 제 옆에서 무언가 뚝 부러지는 소리를 들었습니다. 그리고 제 머릿속의 목소리가 말했습니다, 빌어먹을 연필! 저는 몸을 돌려 스펜서 샤프(Spencer Sharp)를 봤습니다. 그는 끝이 부러진 연필을 쥐고 있었습니다.

스펜서는 우리 반에서 가장 똑똑한 아이입니다. 그는 제가 계산기로 간신히 할 수 있는 계산을 암산으로 합니다. "잭!" 스노드그라스 선생님이 소리쳤습니다. "부디, 자기 시험지만 보렴!"

"죄송해요." 제가 말했습니다.

저는 제 자리에 다시 앉아서 침을 꿀꺽 삼켰습니다. 제 머릿속의 목소리는 스펜서의 것이었습니다! 그 모든 정답은 제가 기억해 낸 것이 아니었습니다. 제가 크럼프 선생님이 하는 말을 들었던 것처럼 저는 스펜서의 목소리를 들었던 것입니다. 그리고 이제 저는 무슨 일이 일어나고 있는지 알았습니다. 그 모든 일은 제가 감전되면서 시작된 것이었습니다.

맙소사(Holy guacamole)! 저는 사람들의 마음을 읽을 수 있었어요!

이것은 제가 스펜서 샤프에게서 시험 정답을 가져오고 있었다는 뜻이었습니다. 그의 시험지를 본 게 아니라, 그의 마음속을 들여다보면서 말이에요!

질문이 있어요: 다른 사람의 마음을 읽는 것이 부정행위인가요? 저는 그것에 대해 썩 확신이 들지 않았습니다. 하지만 신중을 기하기 위해서, 저는 더 이상 듣지 않기로 마음먹었습니다.

저는 콧노래를 불러 봤습니다. 그리고 남은 시험을 혼자 힘으로 끝내려고 최선을 다했습니다. 대양에 관한 문제를 푸는 동안 저는 비치 보이스(Beach Boys)의 노래를 흥얼거렸습니다. 그것은 아빠가 좋아하는 "파도를 타자(Catch a Wave)"라는 노래였습니다. 그

런데도, 저는 스펜서가 정답을 말하는 소리를 완전히 들리지 않게 할 수는 없었습니다.

"누군가 콧노래를 부르는 것 같구나." 스노드그라스 선생님이 말했습니다. "잭, 네가 그러는 거니?"

"어, 아마도요." 제가 말했습니다.

"음, 그러면, 조용히 하렴."

"네, 선생님." 제가 말했습니다.

우림에 대한 질문에서, 저는 우리가 주간 캠프(day camp)에서 불렀던 노래를 흥얼거렸습니다. "존 제이콥 징글하이머-슈미트(John Jacob Jingleheimer-Schmidt)."

"잭!" 스노드그라스 선생님이 소리쳤습니다. "콧노래를 그만두지 않으면, 지금 당장 나에게 시험지를 주고 교실을 떠나야 할 거다."

"죄송해요, 선생님." 제가 말했습니다. "이제 안 그럴게요."

저는 머릿속으로만 흥얼거리려고 노력했습니다. 그렇지만 남은 수업 시간 내내, 스펜서의 생각들이 계속해서 제 흥얼거림 사이로 흘러들어 왔습니다.

"자, 시간 다 됐다." 스노드그라스 선생님이 말했습니다.

저는 제가 A를 받았을 거라고 확신했습니다. 하지만 이상한 느낌이 들었습니다. 저는 이 독심술이 골칫거리가 되리라는 것을 알았습니다.

얼마나 큰 골칫거리일지는, 곧 알게 될 것이었습니다.

4장

학교가 거의 끝났습니다. 저는 책가방을 가지러 교실로 들어갔습니다. 콜먼-레빈 선생님은 돼지 뇌가 올라가 있는 책상에 앉아 있었습니다. 그녀는 제가 마음을 읽을 수 있다는 것을 모릅니다! 저는 교실에 있는 다른 친구들을 빙 둘러봤습니다. 그들 중 누구도 제 능력을 알지 못합니다!

제가 고개를 돌리자, 라디오 손잡이를 맞추는 것 같았습니다. 잡음으로 나뉘어져, 아이들이 생각하는 것이 조금씩 조금씩 저에게 들어왔습니다:

. . . 숙제가 이렇게나 많다니 믿을 수 없어. . .

. . . 점심으로 먹은 피자가 아직도 뱃속에 걸려 있어. . .

저는 이런 것들을 누가 생각하고 있는지는 구별할 수 없었습니다. 하지만 저는 그것이 모두 교실에 있는 아이들에게서 나오는 말이라는 것을 알았습니다.

문이 열리고, 관리인, 플로이드 호그마이스터(Floyd Hogmeister) 아저씨가 들어왔습니다. 우리 반 아이들은 그를 좀 무서워합니다. 어떤 사람들은 뒤통수에도 눈이 달려 있다고 사람들이 말하기도 하잖아요? 네, 그게 바로 호그마이스터 아저씨입니다. 그는 그 어떤 것 하나도 놓치지 않습니다 ― 특히 어떤 아이가 하면 안 되는 일을 하고 있는 경우에 말이에요.

"콘센트에 문제가 있다고 들었는데요." 그가 콜먼-레빈 선생님에게 말했습니다.

"맞아요, 플로이드 씨." 그녀가 말했습니다. "잭이 아까 오전에 감전됐을 때 그것을 차단시킨 게 틀림없어요. 당신이 그것을 교체해야 할 것 같아요."

"제가 잠깐 살펴보죠." 그가 말했습니다.

관리인 아저씨는 제가 감전됐을 때 터져 버린 콘센트를 점검하러 갔습니다. 그가 그 일을 하는 동안, 저는 교실을 훑어봤습니다. 저는 사람들이 생각하고 있는 이런저런 것들을 더 들어보려고 했습니다:

. . . 엄마가 학교 끝나고 사탕을 너무 많이 먹지 말라고 하셨는데. 1파운드 (약 0.45킬로그램) 정도면 너무 많은가? . . .

. . . 나는 그 지리 시험에서 F를 받게 될 거야. 그러면 아빠가 난리를 치시겠지. . .

. . . 죽이자. 오늘 죽일까? 지금 죽일

까? 아냐! 내일 죽이자! . . .

워! 이게 뭐였죠? 제가 제대로 들은 게 맞나요? 저는 고개를 흔들었습니다. 그런 다음 저는 교실을 다시 훑어봤습니다.

. . . *만약에 내가 스펜서를 집으로 초대하면, 그는 내가 자기 숙제를 베끼게 해 줄지도 몰라.* . .

. . . *이 속옷을 입은 게 오늘이 8일째인가, 아니면 7일밖에 안 됐던가? 내일은 꼭 깨끗한 것으로 입어야지.* . .

. . . *죽이고 싶어. 지금은 죽일 수 없어. 내일까지 기다리자. 내일 죽이자!* . . .

또 들렸습니다! 누가 이것을 생각하고 있는 걸까요? 저는 책가방에 책을 다 집어넣었습니다. 그러고 나서 저는 교실을 둘러보았습니다. 저는 아무렇지 않은 척하려고 했습니다. 하지만 그 생각들은 누군가가 살인을 계획하고 있는 것처럼 들렸습니다. 설마 그럴 리가요? 우리 반 아이들 스무 명 중 하나가 정신 나간 사이코(psycho) 살인자일까요?

아뇨, 저는 이 녀석들을 잘 알았습니다. 그들은 멍청한 짓이나, 심지어 역겨운 짓을 할지 몰라요. 하지만 누군가를 죽인다고요? 말도 안 돼요.

그때 제 눈길이 관리인, 호그마이스터 아저씨에게 멈췄습니다. 흐으으으음. 확실히 그는 섬뜩하긴 했습니다. 하지만 살인자일까요?

제가 누구의 생각을 듣고 있는지 저는 전혀 몰랐습니다. 하지만 저는 걱정이 되었습니다. 저는 이것을 선생님에게 확인해 보는 것이 좋겠다고 생각했습니다.

저는 콜먼-레빈 선생님의 책상으로 다가갔습니다. 얼굴을 찡그린 채로, 그녀는 시험지를 채점하고 있었습니다.

"잠깐 말씀 좀 드려도 될까요, 콜먼-레빈 선생님?" 제가 물었습니다.

그녀는 시험지 더미에서 고개를 들지도 않았습니다.

"내가 지금 많이 바쁘구나, 잭." 그녀가 말했습니다.

"죄송해요." 제가 말했습니다. "좀 중요한 일이라서요."

그녀는 정말 큰 한숨을 내쉬었습니다. 콜먼-레빈 선생님은 흔히 말하는 따뜻하고, 부드러운 사람은 아니었습니다.

"그래, 말해 봐." 그녀가 말했습니다.

저는 주위를 둘러봤습니다. 많은 아이들이 저를 바라보고 있었습니다. 호그마이스터 아저씨도 마찬가지였습니다. 그의 두 눈은 마치 그가 제 마음을 읽고 있는 것처럼 저에게 고정되어 있었습니다. 그리고 저는 정말로 그가 말하는 것을 들었습니다, 이 아이가 콘센트를 차단시킨 그 아이로군. 꼬마 말썽꾸러기 같으니. 잘 지켜보는 게 좋겠어.

저는 호그마이스터 아저씨에게 희미하게 미소를 지어 보였습니다. 그러고 나서 저는 다시 콜먼-레빈 선생님에게 고개를 돌렸습니다.

"밖에서 말해도 될까요?" 제가 말했습니다.

"밖에서? 왜 밖에서 말하려는 거니?"

"제가 말해야 하는 게 개인적인 일이라서요." 제가 말했습니다.

"알겠다." 그녀가 말했습니다. "따라오렴."

그녀는 자신의 작업용 부츠를 신은 채 터벅터벅 교실 밖으로 걸어 나갔습니다. 저는 그녀를 따라 복도로 갔습니다.

"무슨 일이니, 잭?"

"먼저, 제가 선생님께 개인적인 질문을 하나 해도 될까요, 콜먼-레빈 선생님?"

"무슨 질문인지에 달려 있지." 그녀가 말했습니다.

"선생님은 초능력(ESP)을 믿으세요?"

"글쎄다." 그녀가 말했습니다. "나는 과학자야. 그래서 나는 편견이 없단다. 그런 것들이 존재할 가능성도 있어. 그건 왜 물어보니?"

"왜냐하면 오늘 제가 마음을 읽어내는 방법을 알게 된 것 같아서요." 제가 말했습니다.

"그렇구나"가 그녀가 말한 전부였습니다.

"저는 교실에 있는 사람들의 생각을 내내 듣고 있어요." 저는 그녀에게 말했습니다. "그리고 믿기 힘든 말이지만, 그들 중 한 사람이 살인을 꾸미고 있는 것 같아요. 내일이요!"

콜먼-레빈 선생님은 저를 아주 심각하게 바라보았습니다.

"네가 살인자의 마음을 읽는다는 말이니?" 그녀가 말했습니다.

저는 고개를 끄덕였습니다. 그러자 그녀는 제 손을 잡았고 토닥거렸습니다. 그것은 전혀 콜먼-레빈 선생님답지 않았습니다.

제 머릿속 어딘가에서 저는 들었습니다, 이 아이는 괴짜(loony toons)로군! 정신이 나갔어.

"네가 이걸 나에게 말해 줘서 기쁘구나, 잭." 그녀가 말했습니다. 그녀는 저에게 굉장히 진심 어린 미소를 지어 보였습니다. "내일, 우리의 눈과 귀를 활짝 열고 지켜보자. 어쩌면 우리는 함께 그게 누구인지 알아내서 그가 살인을 저지르기 전에 그를 막을 수 있을 거야."

"그럼요." 제가 말했습니다.

콜먼-레빈 선생님은 제가 말한 것을 하나도 믿지 않았습니다.

"하지만 일단은." 그녀가 말했습니다. "교실로 돌아가렴."

우리는 다시 들어왔습니다. 잠시 후 종이 울렸고 콜먼-레빈 선생님은 우리를 보내주었습니다.

"자, 모두. 잘 가라." 그녀가 말했습니다. "나는 시체 안치소로 갈 예정이야. 하지만 먼저, 뱀의 식사 시간이란다. 오늘의 메뉴는 육즙이 풍부하고 맛있는 생쥐란다."

콜먼-레빈 선생님은 굉장히 행복한 표정을 하고 있었습니다.

맙소사, 정말 별난 사람이야! 우리가 줄지어 교실을 나가는 동안에 저는 아이들 중 한 사람이 생각하는 것을 우연히 들었습니다. 그녀는 정말로 시체를 자르는 것을 좋아하는구나.

흐으음. 그 말은 저를 생각에 빠지게 했습니다. 어쩌면 콜먼-레빈 선생님은 살아 있는 몸을 자르는 것 또한, 좋아할지도 모릅니다!

5장

집에 돌아왔을 때, 저는 아빠에게 무슨 일이 일어났는지 이야기하기로 했습니다. 우리는 언제나 꽤 친하게 지내왔습니다. 하지만 부모님이 이혼하고, 아빠가 자신만의 아파트를 구한 뒤로 우리는 훨씬 더 친해졌습니다. 저는 아빠에게 무엇이든지 말할 수 있습니다. 그리고 아빠는 언제나 이해해 줍니다.

"난 이해가 되지 않는구나." 아빠가 말했습니다. "네가 사람들의 마음을 읽을 수 있다고 생각한단 말이니?"

"아뇨, 아빠." 제가 말했습니다. "제가 그럴 수 있다고 *생각하는* 게 아니에요. 제가 그럴 수 있다는 걸 저는 알아요."

"미안하지만, 잭." 그는 말했습니다. "그게 가능할 것 같지가 않구나."

"오, 틀림없이, 가능해요." 제가 말했습니다.

"그래 좋다. 내가 바로 지금 무슨 생각을 하고 있지? 바로 지금 이 순간?"

"아빠가 생각하고 있는 건 이거죠." 제가 말했습니다. "아마도 이혼이 결국 저에게 영향을 미치는 것 같다고요. 어쩌면 저를 아동 심리 상담사에게 보내야 할 것 같다고요."

그의 입이 떡 벌어졌습니다.

"그게 바로 내가 하는 생각이라는 걸 어떻게 알았니?" 그는 속삭였습니다.

"아빠, 제가 이미 말했잖아요." 제가 말했습니다. "저는 마음을 읽는다고요. 과학 시간에 그렇게 됐어요. 제가 감전되었거든요."

"좋아, 내가 지금은 무엇을 생각하고 있니?"

"그 상담사가 다음 주 월요일에 시간

이 있기를 바라고 있죠." 제가 말했습니다. "아빠, 믿어 주세요. 이건 이혼하고는 아무런 상관이 없어요."

아빠는 한숨을 쉬었고 고개를 저었습니다.

"이거 굉장하구나." 그가 말했습니다. "정말 굉장해. 좋아, 내가 무슨 숫자를 생각하고 있지?"

"87이요." 제가 말했습니다. "아빠, 저는 제가 학교에서 들은 것에 대해서 아빠의 조언이 필요해요. 누군가가 살인을 계획하고 있다고요."

그는 저를 매우 심각하게 바라보았고 눈을 가늘게 떴습니다.

"내가 무슨 동물을 생각하고 있지?" 그가 물었습니다.

"오리너구리요." 저는 조바심을 내며 말했습니다. "아빠, 제가 한 말 못 들으셨어요? 누군가가 학교에서 살인을 계획하고 있어요."

"미안하다, 잭." 그가 말했습니다. "아들이 독심술사라는 게 정말 너무 믿기 힘든 일이라서 말이야. 하지만 너는 내가 생각하는 걸 모두 맞혔어. 87과 오리너구리까지. 자 누가 살인을 계획하고 있다는 게 다 무슨 말이니?"

"저는 누군가의 생각을 듣게 됐어요. 누군가를 죽이겠다는 생각이었어요. 내일이요. 그 사람이 우리 반 아이들 중 하나일 리는 없어요. 아마 관리

인 아저씨일 거예요. 그는 정말 이상하거든요. 우리가 지하에 있는 그의 사무실 근처에서 서성거릴 때마다, 그는 우리에게 소리를 질러요. 한 번은 우리가 그를 귀찮게 하는 걸 그만두지 않으면, 우릴 죽이겠다고 말한 적도 있어요."

"오, 그건 그냥 말이 그렇다는 거지." 아빠가 말했습니다. "사람들은 그런 말을 곧잘 하잖니. 그렇다고 해서 그들이 살인자라는 건 아니야."

아빠 말도 일리가 있었습니다. 하지만 호그마이스터 아저씨가 아니라면, 그건 누구였을까요? 콜먼-레빈 선생님?

"아빠, 콜먼-레빈 선생님 만나 보셨죠. 그녀가 살인할 사람처럼 보이던가요?"

"당연히 아니지. 너 정말 바보같이 구는구나, 잭." 아빠가 손사래를 치며 말했습니다. 그리고 그는 저에게 시선을 고정했습니다. "좋아, 자. 내가 생각하고 있는 유명한 가수가 누구니? 네가 매번 이걸 할 수 있으면, 나는 너를 *투나잇 쇼(The Tonight Show)*에 내보낼 수 있겠어."

저는 아빠의 말을 무시했습니다. 그는 이것을 진지하게 받아들이지 않는 것이 분명했습니다. 하긴, 그는 그 무서운 목소리가, "죽여. . . 죽여!"라고 말하는 것을 들은 적이 없었으니까요. 어떤 사람의 목숨이 위험에 처해 있었습니다. 그리고 저는 이 수수께끼를 혼자서

해결해야 했습니다. 지금까지 저에게는 주요 용의자가 두 명 있었습니다: 호그마이스터 아저씨와 콜먼-레빈 선생님입니다.

그리고 아빠가 생각하고 있던 유명한 가수가 누구였는지 궁금할까 봐 말하는데, 그것은 배리 매닐로(Barry Manilow)였습니다. 웩!

6장

다음 날 저는 귀마개를 하고 학교에 갔습니다. 그것을 쓴 저는 바보처럼 보였습니다. 하지만 저는 그것이 다른 사람들의 생각을 차단하는 데 도움이 된다는 것을 알게 됐습니다.

마음을 읽는 것의 문제는 이겁니다. 알게 되는 일들 대부분이, 그렇지 않았으면 하는 것이라는 점입니다. 우리 옆집에 사는 나이 많은 여성, 타라다시 부인(Mrs. Taradash)의 경우처럼요. 저는 그녀가 우리 아빠와 데이트하고 싶어 한다는 것을 알게 됐습니다. 오늘 아침에 엘리베이터 안에서 그걸 알게 됐죠. 그리고 아빠의 경우도 그렇죠. 저는 그가 대략 2년 동안 치과에 가지 않았다는 것을 알게 됐습니다. 그는 저를 6개월마다 치과에 가게 하는데요. 이건 불공평해요!

저는 30분 일찍 학교에 도착했습니다. 조금 염탐하려고 그렇게 했습니다. 혼자서 살인자를 추적해야 하는 것은 무서웠습니다. 하지만 제가 달리 무엇을 할 수 있을까요? 저는 경찰에게 갈 수 없었습니다. 제가 그들에게 뭐라고 말하겠어요? 살인을 계획하고 있는 어떤 사람의 마음을 제가 읽었다고요? 왠지 그들은 그 말에 그리 깊은 인상을 받을 것 같지 않았습니다.

저는 귀마개를 벗고, 지하로 내려가서, 관리인 아저씨의 사무실 주변을 서성거렸습니다. 호그마이스터 아저씨가 저의 1순위 용의자였습니다. 그렇게 생각한 가장 큰 이유는 제가 콜먼-레빈 선생님이 1순위 용의자가 아니기를 바랐기 때문입니다. 그녀는 좀 이상하기는 하지만, 저는 그녀가 좋습니다.

저는 밖에서 세차게 내리는 비와 천둥소리를 들을 수 있었습니다. 커다란 폭풍이 몰려오고 있었습니다. 저는 이것을 아침 뉴스에서 들었습니다. 폭풍 때문에 지하가 훨씬 더 무섭게 느껴졌습니다. 하지만 저는 그것 때문에 그만두지는 않았습니다. 저는 살인자가 살인을 저지르기 전에 그가 누구인지 알아내야 했습니다.

저는 복도에서 쓰레기를 줍는 척했습니다. 하지만 저는 호그마이스터 아저씨의 악랄한 생각을 듣기를 바라고 있었죠. 몇 분 동안, 호그마이스터 아저씨는 관심이 갈 만한 생각은 단 하나도 하지 않았습니다. 코가 간지럽군, 저는 들었습니다. 긁어야겠어. 그러고 나서, 으으음, 기분 좋아. 긁는 건 기분 좋아. 특히 간지러울 때. 안 간지러울 때는 이만큼 좋지는 않지. 잠시 후 저는 또 들었습니다. 콘센트. 새 콘센트를 끼워야 해. 그 잭이라는 녀석이 예전 것을 차단 시켰단 말이지. 멍청이 같으니라고!

그러니까 호그마이스터 아저씨는 제가 멍청하다고 생각했다는 거죠, 그렇죠? 뭐, 저도 그가 그렇게 천재라고는 생각하지 않았어요. 그렇지만, 문제는, 그가 살인자인지에 대한 것이었죠.

저는 밖에서 나는 천둥 소리를 몇 번 더 들었습니다.

호그마이스터 아저씨는 저 안에서 뭘 하고 있는 걸까요? 저는 알고 싶었습니다. 문에는 열쇠 구멍이 없었습니다. 하지만 문과 바닥 사이에 아주 작은 공간이 있었습니다. 저는 엎드려서 문 밑으로 자세히 들여다보려고 했습니다.

처음에 저는 아무것도 보지 못했습니다. 그다음 저는 커다란 두 발을 봤습니다. 그리고 그 발은 문 쪽으로 걸어오기 시작했습니다! 오, 안 돼! 저는 어서 일어나야 했습니다!

문이 휙 하고 열렸습니다. 저는 허둥지둥 일어났습니다. 하지만 저는 발을 헛디뎌서 앞으로 넘어지고 말았습니다. 호그마이스터 아저씨는 거인처럼 서서 저를 내려다봤습니다.

천둥이 더 가까이에서 우르릉거렸습니다.

"너 도대체 뭐 하고 있는 거냐?" 그는 정말로 화난 목소리로 말했습니다.

"오, 안녕하세요, 호그마이스터 아저씨." 제가 말했습니다. 저는 일어나서 셔츠와 바지에서 먼지를 탁탁 털어냈습니다.

"내가 말했지, 내 사무실 앞 바닥에 엎드려서 뭐 하고 있냐고?" 그가 따져 물었습니다.

"어, 팔 굽혀 펴기를 했어요, 아저씨." 제가 말했습니다.

"뭐?"

"팔 굽혀 펴기를 하고 있었어요. 저는 항상 수업 전에 팔 굽혀 펴기를 하거든요. 저 자신을 깨우려고요."

호그마이스터 아저씨는 그의 무시무시한 눈을 저에게 고정했습니다. 그러고 나서 그는 몸을 아래로 많이 기울여서 그의 얼굴을 제 얼굴에 가까이 들이댔습니다. 그는 아침으로 마늘 도넛을 먹은 것이 분명합니다. 우. 웩!

저는 그가 망치를 들어 제 머리 위로 쾅 내리칠까 봐 겁이 났습니다. 하지만 대신에 그는 다른 행동을 했습니다. 그는 웃기 시작했습니다. 저는 전에 호그마이스터 아저씨가 웃는 것을 본 적이 없습니다. 그것은 그다지 보기 좋은 광경은 아니었습니다.

그때 저는 그의 생각에 채널을 맞췄습니다. *팔 굽혀 펴기라고! 그만 좀 해라! 저 녀석은 내가 정말 그걸 믿을 거라고 생각하나?* 고개를 저으며, 그는 돌아서서 복도를 따라 걸어갔습니다. *이 녀석들은—정말 웃겨 죽겠구만!* 그는 또다시 이상한 소리로 웃었습니다.

저는 호그마이스터 아저씨가 떠나는 것을 지켜봤습니다. 저는 매우 혼란스러웠습니다. 그의 생각은 살인자의 생각처럼 들리지는 않았습니다. 호그마이스터 아저씨는 이상한 사람입니다, 틀림없어요. 하지만 저는 그를 용의자 목록에서 지워야 할지도 모른다고 생각하기 시작했습니다. 하지만, 제가 그렇게 하면, 그러면 1순위 용의자는. . . 콜먼-레빈 선생님이 됩니다!

7장

교실 바깥에서, 비가 세차게 창문을 때리고 있었습니다. 번개가 번쩍거렸습니다. 천둥이 요란한 소리를 냈습니다. 콜먼-레빈 선생님은 출석을 확인하고 있었습니다. 그리고 그때 저는 어디선가 이상한 목소리를 들었습니다. *죽이자!*

오늘 죽이자!

콜먼-레빈 선생님은 출석 확인을 마쳤습니다. 이제 그녀는 일어나서 제 책상으로 걸어오고 있었습니다. 그녀는 저를 똑바로 바라보고 있었습니다. 저는 들었습니다, *때가 오면 이 녀석을 죽이자! 피 맛이 얼마나 간절한지!*

으악!

"잭." 콜먼-레빈 선생님이 말했습니다. "오늘 점심을 빨리 먹을 수 있겠니? 그러고 나서 곧장 여기 교실로 돌아와 줬으면 좋겠구나." 그녀의 얼굴에 이상한 표정이 스쳤습니다.

"어, 무-무엇 때문에요?" 저는 말을 더듬었습니다.

"너에게 할 말이 있단다."

"그러니까, 단 둘이서만요?" 제가 말했는데, 끽끽하는 소리에 더 가까운 소리가 나왔습니다.

"당연히 단 둘이서 보는 거지." 그녀가 말했습니다. "너를 위한 깜짝 선물이 있단다."

저는 침을 꿀꺽 삼켰습니다. 그 깜짝 선물이 무엇인지 제가 알고 있다는 느낌이 들었습니다. 콜먼-레빈 선생님은 사이코 살인자였고, 제가 그녀의 다음 희생자였던 것입니다. 깜짝 선물이라니요! 저는 여기서 빠져나가야 했습니다. 하지만 어떻게 빠져나가죠?

수학과 지리 수업 사이에 저는 아빠

에게 전화하려고 했습니다. 저는 그가 와서 저를 집으로 데려가기를 바랐습니다. 하지만 제가 아빠에게 전화했을 때는, 그의 자동 응답기가 나왔습니다. 이는 이상한 일이었어요. 아빠는 언제나 집에 있거든요. 그는 작가이고, 집이 그가 일하는 곳입니다. 하지만 오늘, 그 많은 날 중에, 그는 외출 중이었습니다. 저는 그에게 메시지를 남겼습니다. "학교로 와서 저 좀 데려가 주세요!" 저는 말했습니다. "당장이요!"

그러고 나서 저는 크럼프 선생님의 양호실로 갔습니다. 저는 그녀에게 아프다고 말했습니다. 그녀의 양호실에 계속 있으면, 저는 안전할 것입니다. 하지만 그녀는 저의 체온을 재고는 저에게 아무 이상이 없다고 말했습니다. 그녀는 저를 영어 수업으로 돌려보냈습니다.

점심시간에 저는 스펜서 샤프가 앉은 탁자에 앉았습니다. 그리고 저는 그가 다음 달 액션랜드 놀이공원 (Actionland Amusement Park)에서 열리는 자신의 생일 파티에 저를 초대하려고 생각하는 것을 들었습니다. 그것은 정말 좋았을 겁니다. 애석하지만 저는 살아서 그것을 즐기지 못할 수도 있어요.

콜먼-레빈 선생님은 저에게 빨리 먹으라고 말했었죠. 저는 너무 겁이 나서 아무것도 먹을 수가 없었습니다. 폭풍은 이제 아주 거세졌습니다. 12시 30분밖에 되지 않았습니다. 하지만 밤만큼이나 어두워 보였습니다. 그리고 아빠는 아직 나타나지 않았습니다.

저는 위층 교실로 올라가기 두려웠습니다. 그렇지만 저에게는 계획이 있었습니다. 만약 콜먼-레빈 선생님이 뭔든 의심스러운 일을 하면, 저는 비명을 지르고 필사적으로 도망칠 것입니다. 그래요, 이게 뭐 대단한 계획은 아니죠. 그저 제가 압박감을 느끼고 있을 때 생각해 낼 수 있는 최선의 방법일 뿐이었습니다. 하지만 제가 교실에 올라갔을 때, 콜먼-레빈 선생님은 거기 있지도 않았습니다.

교실에 혼자 있는 것은 오싹했습니다. 한쪽 구석에서는, 해골이 저를 향해 웃고 있는 것 같았습니다. 그 또한, 한때 콜먼-레빈 선생님의 학생이었을지도 모릅니다.

저는 제 책상에 앉아서 기다렸습니다. 갑자기 쾅 하고 벼락이 치는 소리가 났습니다. 그 소리가 너무 커서 저는 정말로 공중에 몇 인치쯤 튀어 올랐습니다. 그 후 곧바로, 모든 전등이 나갔습니다.

번개 때문에 전기가 나간 것이 틀림없었습니다. 어두운 교실에서 홀로, 저는 몹시 겁에 질려 있었습니다.

조심스럽게 저는 제 책상에서 일어

났습니다. 번개의 번쩍임으로, 저는 문까지 갈 수 있을 만큼 충분히 잘 볼 수 있었습니다.

그곳에 절반쯤 다다랐을 때, 저는 정말로 오싹한 느낌이 들었습니다. 교실에는 저 혼자만 있는 게 아니라는 느낌 말이에요. 그리고 바로 그 후에, 저는 어떤 생각을 듣게 됐습니다. 그것은 말했습니다, *저기 그가 있다! 이제야 그를 손에 넣었어! 지금이 죽일 때야!*

8장

저는 소리를 지르며 문을 향해 달려갔습니다. 운 나쁘게도, 저는 어둠 속에서 책상에 발이 걸려 넘어졌고 바닥에 세게 고꾸라졌습니다. 고통이 제 무릎을 파고들었습니다.

*그를 죽이자! 지금 그를 죽여!*라는 생각이 제 귀에 들렸습니다.

밖에서 천둥이 다시 커다란 소리를 냈습니다. 그때 저는 울기 시작했습니다. 인정해야겠네요. 저도 어쩔 수 없었어요. 여러분도 저였다면, 그랬을 거예요. 그렇게 생각하지 않는다면, 여러분은 자신을 속이고 있는 겁니다.

그리고 바로 그때 전등이 번쩍거리며 들어왔습니다. 저는 눈부신 빛 속에서 눈을 깜박였습니다. 저는 주위를 둘러보았습니다.

거기에는 아무도 없었습니다. 한 사람도요. 그렇다면 저는 누구의 생각을 들은 것일까요? 이해할 수 없었습니다. 어쩌면 제가 그 말들을 그냥 상상한 것일 수도 있습니다. 그러나 제가 미쳤던 것이라고 생각하려던 참에, 저는 그 생각들을 다시 들었습니다. *그가 걸려들었어. 죽일 준비가 됐다. 지금 그를 삼켜 버리자!*

뭐? 잠깐만요! 그를 삼켜 버리겠다고? 대체 어떤 살인자가 70파운드(약 31.7킬로그램)가 나가는 아이를 삼킬 수 있나요?

곁눈질로, 저는 어떤 빠른 움직임을 보았습니다. 저는 돌아서서 살펴봤습니다. 아무것도 없었습니다. 수조 중 하나에 그냥 물고기 몇 마리가 좀 있었을 뿐입니다. 그리고 그때 저는 다시 살펴봤습니다.

아뇨, 단순한 물고기 몇 마리가 아니었습니다. 피라냐였습니다. 피라냐가 작은 물고기 한 마리를 집어삼키려 하고 있었습니다! 콜먼-레빈 선생님이 점심시간에 피라냐가 있는 수조에 그것을 넣은 것이 분명합니다. 제가 계속 듣고 있었던 것은 피라냐의 생각이었어요!

저는 벌떡 일어나서 피라냐 수조 쪽으로 갔습니다. 피라냐가 작은 물고기를 구석에 몰아넣고 있었습니다. 턱을 크게 벌리고, 그것은 작은 물고기를 꿀꺽 삼키려 하고 있었습니다.

저는 수조를 철썩 쳤습니다. 두 물고기가 튀어 올랐습니다. 저는 물고기 그물을 찾으려고 미친 듯이 주변을 둘러보았습니다. 아, 저기에 하나가 있었습니다. 저는 그것을 피라냐 수조에 집어넣고 조심스럽게 작은 물고기를 건졌습니다. 그러고 나서 저는 그것을 물고기 수조로 가져가 그 안에 퐁당 넣어 주었습니다. 제 손에 물이 튀었습니다.

어디선가 저는 지금까지 들었던 것 중에 가장 조그마한 목소리를 들었습니다. 그것은 말했습니다, 기적이다! 기적이야! 신의 손에 구원받았다!

피라냐 수조 근처의 바닥에는 전기 코드 하나가 빠져 있었습니다. 수조 안의 여과 장치 모터를 돌리는 전선이었습니다. 제가 피라냐의 주의를 돌리려고 수조를 쳤을 때 당겨져서 빠진 것이 틀림없습니다. 저는 허리를 숙여서 그것을 다시 꽂았습니다. 저는 제 손이 젖어 있다는 것을 잊고 있었습니다.

파란 불꽃이 일었습니다. 제 손은 팔까지 온통 따끔거렸습니다. 눈에서는 폭죽이 터졌습니다.

그런 다음 저는 정신을 잃었습니다.

9장

정신을 차렸을 때, 저는 다시 양호실 침대 위에 있었습니다. 크럼프 선생님과 콜먼-레빈 선생님이 저를 내려다보고 있었습니다. 아빠도요.

"오, 안녕하세요." 제가 말했습니다.

"내가 교실 바닥에 있는 너를 발견했단다." 콜먼-레빈 선생님이 말했습니다. "좀 어떠니?"

"괜찮아요, 감사합니다." 저는 말했습니다. 아뇨, 이번에는 사실대로 말해야겠어요. "사실은, 별로 안 괜찮아요." 저는 말했습니다.

"넌 우리를 상당히 놀라게 했어, 잭." 아빠가 말했습니다.

"죄송해요." 제가 말했습니다. "두 번이나 감전되다니 바보 같죠, 그렇죠?"

"네가 괜찮아서 다행이야." 콜먼-레빈 선생님이 말했습니다.

저는 간신히 웃어 보였습니다. 결국에는 저는 제 담임 선생님이 사이코 살인자가 아니라는 것이 기뻤습니다. 저는 일어나 앉았습니다.

"그래서 무슨 일로 저를 보고 싶어 하신 거예요?" 제가 물었습니다. "깜짝 선물이 뭐였나요?"

"아, 그거." 그녀는 말했습니다. "방학 동안에 학생 한 명이 우리 타란툴라를 돌보게 해야겠다고 내가 결정했거든.

모두의 이름을 가지고 추첨했지. 그리고 어떻게 됐게? 네가 당첨됐단다!"

"어... 좋네요... 좋은 것 같아요." 제가 말했습니다.

그러니까 그게 큰 깜짝 선물이었던 거군요. 타란툴라를 돌보게 된 것이요. 뭐, 사이코 살인자에게 죽는 것보다는 낫지만요.

"좋아." 콜먼-레빈 선생님이 말했습니다. "나는 그게 너를 기쁘게 할 거라고 생각했단다. 하지만, 중요한 건, 네가 무사하다는 거지." 그녀는 다시 제 손을 토닥거렸습니다.

저는 그녀가 실제로는 무엇을 생각하는지 들어보려고 기다렸습니다. 아무것도 들리지 않았습니다. 무슨 일이 일어난 거죠?

그리고 그때 저는 번뜩 깨달았습니다. 두 번째로 전기 충격을 받은 것이 제 마음 읽기 능력을 사라지게 한 것이 틀림없습니다. 그런 일이 가능할까요? 저는 확인해 봐야 했습니다.

"아빠." 제가 말했습니다. "1부터 10까지의 숫자 가운데 하나를 생각해 보세요. 빨리요."

"그래, 알았다." 그가 말했습니다. 그는 크럼프 선생님과 콜먼-레빈 선생님을 향해 돌아섰습니다. "잘 보세요." 그가 말했습니다. "잭은 마음을 읽을 수 있답니다. 정말 놀라워요."

"진심은 아니시겠죠." 크럼프 선생님이 말했습니다.

"저는 완전히 진심입니다." 아빠가 말했습니다. "보세요."

"아빠가 생각하는 숫자는... 5예요." 제가 말했습니다.

"아니야." 아빠가 말했습니다.

그는 저를 쳐다보고 어리둥절해서 얼굴을 찌푸렸습니다.

"보통은 한 번에 맞힌답니다." 아빠가 말했습니다.

"아빠가 생각하는 숫자는... 10이에요."

"아니야." 아빠가 말했습니다. 아빠는 조금 당황한 것 같았습니다.

"아빠가 생각하는 숫자는... 3인가요?"

"아니야." 아빠가 말했습니다.

"1?"

"아니야."

"7?"

"아니야. 잭, 어떻게 된 거니?"

"6?"

"아니야."

"8?"

"아니야. 잭, 이게 무슨 일이니?"

"아빠, 제 능력이 사라진 것 같아요." 제가 말했습니다.

"여러분이 어제 잭을 봤어야 했는데." 아빠가 말했습니다.

크럼프 선생님과 콜먼-레빈 선생님
은 그저 고개를 끄덕일 뿐이었습니다.
그리고 저는 그들의 생각을 들을 수는
없었지만, 그들이 저와 아빠가 미쳤다
고 생각하고 있다는 것을 꽤 확신해요.
　아무튼 저는 더 이상 독심술사가 아
니고, 저는 그것이 딱히 아쉽지는 않았
습니다. 어쨌거나, 그리 많이 아쉽진 않
아요. 마음을 읽는 것은 삶을 너무 복
잡하게 합니다. 이제 저는 사람들이 말
하는 것이 그들의 진심이라고 그저 믿
어야 할 겁니다.
　그리고, 이제 더는 스펜서 샤프의 마
음속에서 정답을 들을 수 없으니, 저는
다음 주 영어 시험을 위해서 정말로 공
부를 해야 할 겁니다.

Chapter 1

1. B Have you ever wished you could read people's minds? Tune into their heads and hear exactly what they're thinking? Well, forget it. You wouldn't like it. I know. I did it. And it wasn't a big treat at all. Believe me.

2. B Science is probably my favorite subject. It teaches you stuff that is at least as weird as reading minds.

3. C Mrs. Coleman-Levin is my science teacher. She's also my homeroom teacher. She's kind of weird, but not in a bad way. For one thing, she always wears work boots. Even in summer. Even at dress-up parties at school in the evening. For another thing, she works weekends at the morgue. She does autopsies.

4. A Our classroom has a lot of weird, interesting stuff in it. There's a complete human skeleton hanging in the corner. Not a plastic model, either. It's a real one. On her desk, Mrs. Coleman-Levin keeps a glass jar with a pig brain in it. And we have lots of class pets. But not the cute, furry kind. We have a piranha fish and a tarantula and a snake.

5. D By accident, one of the wires fell into a beaker of water. Without thinking, I reached in and pulled it out. Suddenly my hand got all tingly.

Chapter 2

1. C "How are you feeling, dear?" said a strange, echoey voice. It was the school nurse, Mrs. Krump. Her voice doesn't usually echo.

2. B "Fine, thanks," I said. I always answer "Fine, thanks," even when I'm not. I've found that when people ask you how you are, they don't really want to know. They only want you to say you're fine so they can get on to the next thing.

3. C Although her lips didn't move, I thought I heard Mrs. Krump say, Stupid klutz. You're lucky you didn't electrocute yourself.

4. D I don't know how she did it. Maybe she was a ventriloquist. "How did you do that?" I asked. "How did I do what?" "Say what you just said without

moving your lips."

5. A She made me lie down for fifteen minutes. She stuck a thermometer in my mouth. Then she said, "Zack, you do not have any fever. And you don't seem to be badly hurt. Would you like to go on to your next class?"

Chapter 3

1. A I like geography a lot. But we were having this big test that day. And I forgot to take my geography book home with me to study. So I was pretty much out of luck. Our geography teacher, Mr. Snodgrass, passed out sheets with the test questions. I took a look at mine and started feeling dizzy.

2. C Then I heard a voice inside my head. It said, Tigress and you Fraidies. That was it! The two biggest rivers in Iraq were the Tigris and the Euphrates! But how did I remember it? I quickly wrote down the answers. I looked at the second question. "What is the tallest mountain in the world?" I was about to skip it. But then the answer popped inside my head again. Just like the last time. Mount Everest.

3. B At that exact moment I heard a snapping sound next to me. And the voice inside my mind said, Darn pencil! I turned around to see Spencer Sharp. He was holding a pencil with a broken point.

4. D Question: Is reading somebody's mind cheating? I wasn't too sure about that. But just to be on the safe side, I decided not to listen anymore.

5. A I tried to hum only in my head. But for the rest of the class, Spencer's thoughts kept bleeding through my humming.

Chapter 4

1. D As I turned my head, it was like tuning the knob on a radio. Little bits of what the kids were thinking came to me, separated by static: . . . I can't believe how much homework I have . . . . . . That pizza I had for lunch is still stuck in my stomach . . . I couldn't tell who was thinking these things. But I knew it was all coming from kids in the room.

ANSWER KEY

2. B You know how they say some people have eyes in the back of their heads? Well, that's Mr. Hogmeister. He doesn't miss a thing—especially if a kid is doing something he shouldn't.

3. D But those thoughts sounded like somebody was plotting a murder. Could that be? Was one of the twenty kids in our class a crazy psycho killer? No, I knew these guys. They might do stupid things, or even gross stuff. But kill somebody? No way.

4. A "I've been listening to the thoughts of people in the classroom," I told her. "And I know this will sound unbelievable, but I think one of them is plotting a murder. Tomorrow!"

5. C Then she took my hand and patted it. That is not like Mrs. Coleman-Levin at all. From somewhere inside my head I heard, This kid is loony toons! Crazy as a bedbug. "I'm glad you told me this, Zack," she said. She was giving me this really sincere smile. "Tomorrow, let's keep our eyes and ears open. Maybe together we can discover who it is and stop him before he kills."

Chapter 5

1. B When I got home, I decided to tell my dad what had happened. We've always been pretty close. But we've become even closer since my folks split up, and Dad got his own apartment. I can tell my dad anything at all. And he always understands.

2. A "Here is what you're thinking," I said. "Maybe the divorce is finally getting to me. Maybe you ought to send me to that child psychologist." His mouth dropped open. "How did you know that's what I was thinking?" he whispered.

3. C "I'm sorry, Zack," he said. "It's just pretty incredible to find out your son is a mind reader. But you nailed everything I was thinking. Including the eighty-seven and the duck-billed platypus."

4. D "Maybe it's the janitor. He's very weird. Anytime we hang around his office in the basement, he yells at us. Once he said if we didn't stop bothering

him, he'd kill us." "Oh, that's just an expression," said my dad. "People say that kind of thing all the time. It doesn't mean they're killers."

5. C Somebody's life was in danger. And I was going to have to solve this mystery on my own.

Chapter 6

1. C I came to school wearing earmuffs the next day. I looked stupid in them. But I found it helped block out other people's thoughts.

2. A I got to school half an hour early. That was so I could snoop around a little.

3. B I pretended to be picking up litter in the hallway. But I was hoping to pick up evil thoughts from Mr. Hogmeister. For several minutes, Mr. Hogmeister didn't have a single interesting thought. My nose itches, I heard. I'll scratch it.

4. B What was Mr. Hogmeister doing in there? I wished I could see. There was no keyhole in the door. But there was a little space between the door and the floor. I lay down and tried to peer under the door.

5. D He started laughing. I had never seen Mr. Hogmeister laugh before. It was not a pretty sight. Then I tuned in on his thoughts. Push-ups! Give me a break! Does he really expect me to believe that? He turned and walked down the hallway, shaking his head. These kids—they kill me! He laughed a weird laugh again.

Chapter 7

1. D "Zack," said Mrs. Coleman-Levin, "could you eat lunch quickly today? Then I want you to come right back up here to the classroom." There was a strange expression on her face. "Uh, wh-what for?" I stuttered. "I need to talk to you." "Alone, you mean?" I said, only it came out more like a squeak. "Of course alone," she said.

2. B Between math and geography classes I tried to phone Dad. I wanted him to come and take me home. But when I called him, his answering machine

came on. Which is weird. My dad is always home. He's a writer, and that's where he works. But today, of all days, he was out.

3. A   Then I went to Mrs. Krump's office. I told her I felt sick. If I stayed in her office, I'd be safe. But she took my temperature and said there was nothing wrong with me.

4. D   If Mrs. Coleman-Levin pulled anything funny, I would scream and run for my life. OK, so this wasn't a great plan. It was just the best one I could think of under pressure.

5. C   There was a sudden clap of thunder. It was so loud I actually jumped a couple of inches into the air. Right after that, all the lights went out. Lightning must have knocked out the power.

Chapter 8

1. B   And just then the lights flickered on. I blinked in the glare. I looked around. No one was there. Not a soul.

2. C   He's trapped. Ready for the kill. Swallow him now! What? Wait a minute! Swallow him? What kind of killer could swallow a seventy-pound kid?

3. A   I looked wildly around for a fishnet. Ah, there was one. I stuck it into the piranha tank and gently scooped up the little fish. Then I carried him to the fish tank and plopped him into it.

4. D   From somewhere I heard the teeniest voice I've ever heard. It said, A miracle! A miracle! Saved by the hand of God!

5. D   On the floor near the piranha tank was a loose electric cord. It ran the filter motor in the aquarium. It must have yanked free when I slapped the tank to distract the piranha. I bent down and plugged it back in.

Chapter 9

1. C   "You gave us quite a scare there, Zack," said my dad. "I'm sorry," I said. "Pretty dumb of me to electrocute myself twice, huh?" "I'm glad you're OK," said Mrs. Coleman-Levin.

2. B   "So what did you want to see me for?" I asked. "What was the surprise?"
"Oh, that," she said. "I decided to let a student take care of our tarantula over the vacation. I put everyone's name in a hat. And guess what? You won!"

3. C   Getting shocked a second time must have knocked out my mind-reading powers.

4. D   He turned to Mrs. Krump and Mrs. Coleman-Levin. "Watch this," he said. "Zack can read minds. It's amazing."

5. A   So I'm not a mind reader anymore, and I don't really miss it. Not that much, anyway. Mind reading complicates your life too much.

지직! 나는 마음을 읽을 수 있어요
(ZAP! I'm a Mind Reader)

초판 발행   2020년 3월 13일

지은이   Dan Greenburg
기획   이수영
책임편집   정소이
편집   박새미 배주윤
콘텐츠제작및감수   롱테일북스 편집부
저작권   김보경
마케팅   김보미 정경훈

펴낸이   이수영
펴낸곳   (주)롱테일북스
출판등록   제2015-000191호
주소   04043 서울특별시 마포구 양화로 12길 16-9(서교동) 북앤빌딩 3층
전자메일   helper@longtailbooks.co.kr
(학원·학교에서 본 도서를 교재로 사용하길 원하시는 경우 전자메일로 문의주시면
자세한 안내를 받으실 수 있습니다.)

ISBN 979-11-86701-57-7 14740

롱테일북스는 (주)북하우스 퍼블리셔스의 계열사입니다.

이 도서의 국립중앙도서관 출판시도서목록(CIP)은 서지정보유통지원시스템 홈페이지(http://seoji.nl.go.kr)와
국가자료공동목록시스템(http://www.nl.go.kr/kolisnet)에서 이용하실 수 있습니다. (CIP 제어번호 : CIP2020009047)